FANTASTIC
SELLING

The 10 Undeniable
Traits of Rock-Star,
Top-Producing,
Quota-Busting Salespeople

MEREDITH OLIVER

For information or bulk orders, contact:
meredith@creatingwow.com or call 866-227-9769

www.MeredithCommunications.com

Text Editing by Alison Netsel
Cover Design by Chris Campbell of Dyna Interactive
Interior Design by Adina Cucicov, Flamingo Designs

ISBN 978-0-9978260-4-3

Also by Meredith Oliver

FANtastic Marketing: Leverage Your Fan Factor, Build a Blockbuster Brand, Score New Customers, and Wipe Out the Competition

Click Power: The Proven System Home Builders Use to Drive More Traffic, Leads, and Sales

For Allen,
from the very first time we spoke on the phone,
I knew you were the one sale that I had to close.
Turns out you didn't need a lot of convincing.

Table of Contents

About the Author

A SALES AND MARKETING STRATEGIST, Meredith Oliver is the founder and creative director of Meredith Communications, a digital marketing agency located in Raleigh, North Carolina. Meredith Communications is in its fifteenth year of delivering innovative and effective digital marketing solutions, including website design, search engine optimization, and social media marketing.

Meredith holds a Master's Degree in Communication Technology from Rollins College, a Bachelor's Degree in Psychology from the University of Central Florida, and the prestigious designation of Certified Speaking Professional®, the highest designation conferred by the National Speakers Association.

The author of three books, Meredith has written 1) *Click Power: The Proven System Home Builders Use to Drive More Traffic, Leads, and Sales,* 2) *FANtastic Marketing: Leverage Your Fan Factor, Build a Blockbuster Brand, Score New Customers, and Wipe Out the Competition,* and 3) *FANtastic Selling: The 10 Undeniable Traits of*

Rock-Star, Top-Producing, Quota-Busting Salespeople. All three books are available online and at her seminars.

On the professional speaking circuit since 2001, Meredith has presented her sales and marketing wisdom to audiences ranging in size from 10 to 2,000. She has been a featured speaker at pivotal industry events such as the International Builders Show and the Annual Conference and Expo of the National Automobile Dealers Association.

Meredith is a member of the American Marketing Association, the National Association of Home Builders, the American Society of Association Executives, and the National Speakers Association. Her leadership positions have included President of the National Speakers Association Carolinas Chapter, Chair of the National Association of Home Builders (NAHB) Institute of Residential Marketing, and Chair of the NAHB Professional Women in Building Council Communications and Education Committee. Currently, Meredith sits on the Board of Governors for the NAHB National Sales and Marketing Council and serves as Vice President of Communications of the American Marketing Association Triangle Chapter.

In January 2016, Meredith was honored by the NAHB Professional Women in Building Council as the National Member of the Year. In 2015, she was honored with the Bill Molster Award for Outstanding Service & Lifetime Achievement by the NAHB National Sales and Marketing Council. In 2013, Meredith was named Chapter Member of the Year by the National Speakers Association Carolinas Chapter.

FANTASTIC SELLING

Meredith lives in Raleigh, North Carolina, with her husband, son, and three shih tzus. She is a Florida Gator fan and high-heel shoe fanatic who loves to geek out over technology and digital marketing almost as much as she likes to shop.

Acknowledgements

A BOOK ON SALES DOES not write itself. While I was the one who took the time to write the manuscript, this book is a combination of my experiences with master salespeople and the sales education I've received from the sales leaders who took the time to teach and coach me throughout my career.

No one has taught me more about selling than my dear friend John Palumbo. John is an author, educator, and mentor to salespeople worldwide on the art of influence and persuasion. More than a professional colleague, he is a personal friend who will always answer the phone—no matter where he is around the globe—and give you FANtastic advice, encouragement, or a reason to laugh.

My dear friend Melinda Brody is the most persistent closer you will ever meet. Melinda taught me the dogged art of follow-up. She does not stop calling and emailing until you buy, die, or get a restraining order. I love that about her. For more than a decade, Melinda, John, and I have spoken together in a sales rally roadshow and each time they speak (even though I've heard the talk dozens of times) I learn something new about sales.

Kerry Mulcrone, is a thirty-year sales and sales-management coach, author, and another dear personal friend and colleague, who has taught me how to marry thoughtfulness and follow-up. Her little gift packages and love notes arrive without fail all year long and cheerfully say, "I'm thinking about you." She knows how to stay in front of a decision maker in a friendly, thoughtful way, better than anyone I know. I learned that sales skill from her.

My best friend, life partner, and business partner, Allen Oliver is a FANtastic salesperson who taught me the art of understated, patient selling. I remember on our second date telling him I was very busy and didn't have a lot of time for him. He smiled and nodded and said, "We'll make it work." The next thing I knew I had blown off all my responsibilities the following day and was hanging out with him. Eighteen years later, it still works that way. He brings a richness and fun factor to our lives that I could never supply. And despite all my protestations, he manages to close me in a quiet, patient way every single time.

Special thanks goes to Chris Campbell for the cover design. We've created a lot of cool websites together over the years and I'm so proud of our portfolio of work. You are so busy with our client projects that I tried to use another graphic designer for the cover design, but that was a miserable failure. They just don't know me like you do! You nailed my vision in one draft. I guess you are stuck with me.

Thank you to Alison Netsel for editing the manuscript. You worked quickly and were very easy to work with. You are a FANtastic writer in your own right and our clients love your blog articles. The funny thing is we've been working together for several years and have never spoken on the phone or met in person.

Similarly, this is the eighth book I've published with the interior graphic design by Adina Cucicov of Flamingo Designs. I found her online searching for an interior book designer and liked her portfolio. I've never met her in person either. The one time I deviated from using Adina, the interior design was such a disaster I ended up giving the project to her to fix.

One of my favorite quotes is by Charlie Tremendous Jones, who says, "You will be the same person in five years except for the people you meet and the books you read along the way." I couldn't agree more. I certainly wouldn't be the person I am today without the people I've met and the books I've read. I hope the salespeople in my seminars and workshops have learned as much from me as I have learned from you. I hope this book provides you the insight and knowledge to make a difference in your career and that I can be one of the people who makes a difference to you five years from now.

Thank you to all of you for contributing to my journey.

Introduction

I LOVE A GREAT SALESPERSON. I love experiencing their skills in action—the enthusiasm for the product, the smoothness of the pitch, the subtle calls to action, the bravado it takes to ask for the sale. I love everything about sales, selling, and salespeople. And it's from that perspective that I am writing this book.

I was born to sell. I can't seem to stop selling. Even when I'm trying to dial it down and be less *salesy*, I can't seem to stop. To me there is nothing more fun than pitching a product or service that I truly believe in and convincing someone that they can't live without it. Even now as you read this book, I am hoping to convince you of the value of the concepts, ideas, skills, and attitudes herein. I hope to never stop selling, and since I am a wife, mom, aunt, and daughter, I don't think that will happen anytime soon!

Every member of your organization, no matter how big or small, is in sales and all of them can benefit from learning the 10 undeniable traits of rock-star, top-producing, quota-busting salespeople found within the pages of this book. One of my favorite books is *Selling Is a Team Sport*[1] by Eric Baron. In this ground-breaking book Baron states the following:

> *The old sales paradigm: Research & Development developed the product; the sales force sold the product. The new sales paradigm: the sales force, Research & Development, executives, web developers, accountants, lawyers, inventory clerks—all of your employees—sell the product.*
>
> *Selling is more about fulfilling the true needs of the customer than it is about selling canned pitch. Learning how to recognize and respond to the customer's unspoken needs is the most important step toward becoming a problem-solving seller.*

Every interaction with a customer—whether an internal customer or external customer—either re-sells or un-sells the customer on the value of your product or service. It's really that simple.

While this book is bursting with practical ideas and skills you can learn, the focus of this book is on you—the salesperson. It is a personal development book meant to help you become the best salesperson you can be. I think you'll find many of the concepts will apply to your personal life as well. This book is meant to read as if we are having a one-on-one conversation and the goal of the book is to spark ideas on how you can implement FANtastic Selling ideas into your daily work routines.

How do I know these strategies work? I've held many sales positions throughout the years and have been recognized many times as a top producer in my field. My first sales job was right out of college and I sold Health Management Organizations

(HMOs) to physicians. My official title was Provider Relations Representative, and it was my job to convince popular, well-respected physicians to be preferred providers for the HMO. It was a brutal sale. I had to get past the gatekeeper, score a meeting with the physician (most often in a hallway between his/her appointments), negotiate fees, get a signature (again most often as the physician walked from patient room to patient room), and then manage the very tenuous relationship as claims were processed (often incorrectly) throughout the life of the contract.

After several years of HMO sales, I went to graduate school and earned a Master's Degree in Communication Technology. I then transitioned to an Internet Sales Counselor position with a company (at that time) named Homebuilder.com. This occurred right in the middle of the dot-com boom in the late 90s and early 2000s. This sales job involved me convincing new-construction home builders that the internet was here to stay and they needed to start moving dollars from print advertising to digital advertising. It was a tough sale since most of them didn't even have websites yet. I excelled at the position because I am so passionate about the power of digital marketing and eventually became the Sales Manager for the East Coast of Florida.

My next and current sales position involves selling myself! Once you've sold HMOs to physicians and internet marketing to home builders, selling yourself is a piece of cake. For the last fifteen years, my family's lifestyle and my son's future have depended on my ability to sell the services of Meredith Communications. I wear a lot of hats in our organization, from President to Creative Director, but the one I enjoy the most is CSO—Chief Sales Officer.

I hope within the pages of this book you will find the inspiration, the education, and the motivation to engage in the art and science of FANtastic Selling.

rel·e·vant

closely connected or appropriate to the matter at hand

Are you a Gutenberg printing press
in an Amazon.com world?

I WAS NOT IN THE market for a new dog. It was the absolute farthest thing from my mind. I already had two healthy, happy dogs. I'm a working mom of an elementary age boy who is active in many sports. I run my own business and I travel a lot for work. I needed another dog like I needed a new pair of shoes. And yet Hershey is sleeping peacefully at my feet while I write this book. Here's the rest of the story...

One particular Wednesday, I was scrolling through Facebook when I noticed Jen B., the Online New Homes Specialist for Rose and Womble Realty, using Facebook Live to feature a shelter pet of the week at the Norfolk, Virginia SPCA. Jen's job is to field all of the online requests for information from the Rose and Womble Realty website, respond immediately, and through a series of email and phone conversations set an appointment for the buyer to meet with an onsite sales representative at one of the new home communities they represent. Jen is so good at her job that in January 2016, at The National Awards in Las Vegas, NV, she was recognized as the National Sales and Marketing Council's Online Consultant of the Year, a national award bestowed annually to one online sales counselor in the home building industry.

One of the tactics Jen uses to brand herself and her company in the community is to marry her passion for rescue dogs with real estate. Once a week she features a pet of the week on Facebook Live and treats the pet to a tour of a local new home community while she gives the audience a preview of the model home. It's a win-win. The dog gets exposure to possible adoptive parents, and the home builder's community receives exposure as a great place to live. To my great surprise on this particular Wednesday, Jen was featuring a five-year-old shih tzu (my favorite dog breed) who had been surrendered a couple of weeks prior. I watched the broadcast live and commented on how cute he was.

A couple of days later I emailed Jen about another matter and mentioned in my email that if I were local I would be there in a flash to adopt Hershey. Jen recognized my buying signal in the email and went for the close! She replied to my email with, "You know, if you want to adopt Hershey, I can probably make it happen! Maybe I could even do the paperwork for you and meet you halfway between Raleigh and Norfolk."

That was all the permission and prompting I needed. The next thing I knew, I was watching the video over and over and totally in love with a dog I'd never met. I discussed it with my husband and within a couple of hours of my unrelated email to Jen, I gave her the green light to start the adoption process. As it turned out she was not allowed to do the paperwork and drive him to me, so a few days later we drove three hours to Norfolk, VA, and picked up Hershey. He is a great dog and has absolutely found his forever home.

Jen is one of the most relevant salespeople I've ever met. She knows how to make a relevant emotional connection, she uses a relevant communication channel to get her message out there, and she focuses like a laser beam on the relevant information home buyers are looking for by touring new communities on a weekly basis.

The very first attribute of a rock-star, top-producing, quota-busting FANtastic salesperson is the ability to be relevant. Simply put, are you what your buyers need, when they need it, and how they need it? The authors of *Relevance: The Power to Change Minds and Behaviors and Stay Ahead of the Competition*, Andrea Coville and Paul B Brown, put it this way:

Okay, so what do we mean by relevance? We mean your offering is practical and especially is socially applicable.

We have found that most people misread the definition, putting almost all their emphasis on the practical. That's understandable. It is certainly true that what you are offering must solve a customer need and do it well, but you need to do more. And that is where the emotional part of relevance comes in. If your product/service/

idea resonates with a customer, if it means something to him in addition to being utilitarian, then the relationship will be deeper, longer lasting, and more profitable.

The ability to resonate with customers on an emotional level is the number one skill needed to succeed in today's digitally driven world. We are more connected than ever but we are also more distracted than ever. We have an unlimited amount of information available to us and it is so overwhelming that we actively screen out even the smallest kernel of seemingly irrelevant information. Our brains simply can't hold it all, so we automatically block and filter as much irrelevant information as possible. If your sales pitch, your follow-up, or your presentation fails to resonate with the needs, the wants, the desires, and the emotions of the prospect, you too will be screened out and ignored.

THE INTERNET EMPOWERED BUYER

The art and science of selling has not changed all that much over the years. If you want to sell a product or service, you must do many of the same things we've always done—you have to build rapport, present the features and benefits, build value, overcome objections, and ask for the sale.

So what has changed? The buyers! I recently asked a group of 100 salespeople at a seminar to give me one word to describe today's buyer and they said the following:

- Smart
- Savvy

- Educated
- Opinionated
- Skeptical
- Determined
- Cautious
- Analytical
- Researched
- Demanding
- Resourceful
- Informed
- Knowledgeable
- Discerning
- Hungry
- Discriminating

Do any of these descriptions sound familiar? If this list describes your prospects, leads, and customers, keep reading! This buyer demands relevance or they move on to another salesperson.

With the invention of the internet and social media, today's buyer is empowered by the information available to them online. In the past, buyers had to rely solely on salespeople to learn the information needed to make a buying decision. Think about your own shopping habits. Let's pretend for a moment you are interested in purchasing a new computer. What is your first step? Like 81% of all shoppers you go online before buying to do research.[2] And you don't go to just one website, you visit several, including big-box retailer websites, online review sites, and strictly online retail sites. In fact, more than 70% of shoppers use three or more channels to research a purchase, and between 79% - 82% of consumers use search, brand websites, and customer reviews.[3] You might even post on a social media site and ask for people's recommendations on what type of computer they like or for feedback on a specific model you are considering.

Finally, if you feel really confident in your selection, you will complete the sale online. If you want some additional information, you will visit a retailer in person, armed with your research to gather some final information and make a purchase. This is not the same process we went through twenty years ago. Not by a long shot. If you are the salesperson in the retail location who has the opportunity to work with this shopper, you better be ready with only relevant information and analysis beyond what the buyer could read online. If you don't know as much about the computers for sale in your store as the buyer does, or if you can't add anything of value to the conversation, you will lose the customer's attention, be screened out, and lose the sale.

Do you remember the Terminator movies? In those movies, Arnold Schwarzenegger's character, The Terminator, was a cyborg robot disguised as a human sent back in time to save the planet from an evil machine that was attempting to destroy all mankind. Much of the movie is seen through the eyes of The Terminator. As he encounters new objects and people, his eyes do an analysis and the results display on screen in his mind (think Google Glass without the glasses). Based on the analysis, he makes a decision to save or destroy the object or person and moves on to the next one.

Think of your buyers as The Terminator. No, I'm not suggesting their aim is to destroy you, but I am suggesting that from the moment they meet you—whether it's to discuss buying something for a business or a retail location such as a model home or car dealership—your buyers have the same type of eye scan analysis as The Terminator. They are scanning the landscape, your body language, your appearance, and your first words, to determine if you are going to add value and be relevant to their needs, or if you are going to be a waste of time and they need to abort the mission quickly.

Before you say, *duh*, the fact that the buyer has changed is old news—just wait a moment. I think most salespeople know buyers have changed on an intellectual level. **But the real question is: have you changed your behavior—the way you sell and market—to accommodate the shift?**

ASK YOURSELF THESE QUESTIONS:

- When you first meet with a prospect, how much do you assume they know about your product or service?
- What specifically do you do during the sales conversation to ascertain how much they know or don't know?
- What do you change, edit, delete, or alter in your presentation to account for the information that is already known?
- How much time do you spend before a presentation tailoring the content based on research about the company or individual you are meeting with?
- When you first meet a new prospect, how long do you spend asking questions to get to know them on a personal level?

- How prepared are you to ditch the pitch, set down the brochure, stop the PowerPoint, or abandon the live demo if it is not resonating with the buyer?
- How often do you check in during the sales conversation to determine if you are meeting their needs?

YOUR BUYERS ARE FANS

In addition to being internet empowered, your buyers are already *fans* of your product or service even though they haven't purchased it yet. Fans? How is that possible? They haven't even bought the product or service yet, much less experienced it. Traditionally, the term fan has been applied to happy, satisfied, loyal, existing customers. But I want to change that paradigm in this book and give you another perspective to consider.

Think about it this way: because we do so much online research before we buy, on some level we are already convinced that the product or service is a potential solution to our problem even though we haven't bought it yet. In fact, 80% of buyers know what they want before they even contact a vendor.[4] Internet research is an elimination game, not a selection game. As we do online research we actively eliminate options for a variety of reasons, such as too expensive, too complicated, poor reviews, and/or not a good fit for our needs. We narrow the search down to a couple of possibilities and make a decision from within that group.

Depending on the personality of the shopper and the type of product or service, the research process could take just a few days, but in many cases the research process takes weeks and months. During that time the shopper is becoming more invested in the purchase as they visit your website over and over again. An impression of your company, your products, and your people are forming in their minds and they are beginning to have expectations of what it will be like to do business with you. The shopper has a lot of time and emotion invested in their research process because they want to feel good about the purchase decision. A relationship between the buyer and your product or service has already formed and they haven't even interacted with a human being yet. When the buyer finally does speak to a salesperson, whether it's by phone, live chat, email or in person, he or she feels like they know you. They feel like they know as much about your product as you do. And they certainly would not waste precious time talking to you if they did not think your solution was an answer to their problem.

You may have never thought of it this way, but your prospects, your leads, and your pipeline of future sales are fans. Hence the title of this book, FANtastic Selling. In the FANtastic Selling model, the fans come first. When you put the fans first—when you make the sales conversation about them and not about you and your 300-bullet slide presentation—you become relevant. And relevant salespeople are top-producing, quota-busting, rock-stars.

- What if you started treating your prospects like FANS at a rock concert or sports event?
- What if you started calling your leads and prospects FANS instead of cold terms like "ups" that don't imply a relationship?
- What if you gave your FANS what they want and made it all about them and not about you?

RELEVANT SALESPEOPLE RESONATE

The very first trait of a FANtastic Salesperson is the ability to be **relevant** to your buyers. What does that mean? It means three things: 1) You connect on a relevant emotional level with the prospect; 2) You deliver only relevant information tailored to that buyer; and 3) You harness the power of relevant technology to communicate, market, follow up, and build your brand.

We are going to explore these three skills in much more detail in subsequent chapters. In fact, most of the other traits are meant to support and create relevance. For now, let's explore several practical steps you can take to develop relevance.

1. **Assume a Relationship**—From the first moment you speak to or meet a prospect, assume they know everything about you and are 80% ready to purchase your product and service. At this point, focus the conversation on closing the gap on the last 20% of their decision-making. You can still cover routine information they should know—especially if those details are key to understanding the value of the product— but cover them in a different way, with the assumption that they know them already. Phrases like "You probably saw this on our website" or "You likely read in your research" are extremely effective. They acknowledge the buyer's research process and their knowledge level. That will set them at ease because they know you are in tune with the typical shopping process and you plan to tailor your approach.

2. **Drop the Cliché Sales Questions**—We will talk in more detail in later chapters about questions, but for now I want to make clear that your very first question or statement is of critical importance. Remember my Terminator analogy? Your first question or statement is being scanned on a scale of 1 to 10 on how relevant your approach is to the conversation. Your first question needs to assess what they know, how much they know, and where they've been researching so you can tailor the rest of the conversation to them. Questions like "Have you visited our website?" are a great conversation starter. Eighty to ninety percent will say yes and you can then follow up with "Great! What did you see that prompted you to visit/call/live chat/email me today?"

3. **Be Specific**—Buyers need information that is not readily available online. Your ability to add value to the conversation lies in your ability to be specific about how others have used the product and found it to be a great solution to their needs. You must go beyond the obvious list of features and be able to interpret, analyze, and synthesize the information into a specific solution for their needs. Use statements like "Other buyers have found this feature to be useful", "ABC Company uses it this way..." and "One of my other clients loves this feature because it allows them to..." These statements allow you to give specific examples on how the product is used and why customers like it. This is relevant information and offers behind-the-scenes details that can't

be read on a website, making you extremely valuable to the client's decision-making process.

4. **Do Your Homework**—If your sales role is one where you set appointments with buyers (for example, insurance, financial services, and business-to-business salespeople), then you MUST do your homework on the person and the company before the meeting. In the world of social media, there is no excuse not to at least read the person's LinkedIn profile before the appointment. Study their resume. If you see direct experience related to your product or service, then drop the first 25 slides of your PowerPoint that cover the basic definition of what you are selling. I once had a live demo where the salesperson actually started with the importance of digital marketing. Seriously? You started with statistics on the number of people who use internet marketing with a person who has written three books on the subject and speaks nationally on it? And the person even said "I know you know this but..." and kept going! What a waste of time and frankly it was insulting. I knew immediately that the presentation was canned and not customized to me. Not only do you want to research their background, but of course you are looking for details about them to help build the connection. Tidbits like where they went to school, past employers, and associations they belong to will help you establish rapport and find common ground.

5. **Retire the Sales Funnel**—Your buyers no longer follow a linear path from awareness to purchase. They bounce all over the internet, starting and stopping as they compare features, reviews, pricing, and service options. The buyer's journey (which we will explore in detail later) is a messy squiggly line and your job is to meet them on their journey. Find out what phase of the journey they are in and begin the conversation at that point. The traditional sales funnel or sales process assumes the buyer knows nothing and requires you to follow a prescribed set of steps in a very specific order. To the internet-empowered buyer this approach comes off as canned, scripted, and disingenuous. Don't get me wrong, having a sales process is important. It prevents you from leaving out vital information necessary to the decision-making process and it helps you lead the customer down a metaphorical pathway to a decision. But your sales process can't be so rigid that you always start at the very beginning with the same information. You have to be able to start in the middle if needed and even backtrack to the beginning if you discover they are lacking pieces of vital information.

Being relevant isn't about being hip or cool. You don't have to know the lyrics to the latest pop song on the Top 40 Billboard Charts or understand the inner workings of Minecraft to be relevant to your buyers. I've met some very hip, cool salespeople who were so busy being hip and cool they weren't resonating with their audience in the least. At the same time, having a working understanding of technology and using it to communicate is important. We'll talk more about that in later chapters, but in this trait, I'm not talking about relevance in terms of technology. For my purposes, relevance is about being able to sense where the buyer is in their process and being willing to meet them at that point. It's about stepping out of your comfort zone and focusing on their needs instead of your own performance. It's about asking cogent questions and being able to tailor your presentation on the spot. When you are relevant, you are FANtastic. And when you are FANtastic, the fans love you for it.

FORMULATE YOUR GAME PLAN

Five FANtastic Questions to Help You Become More Relevant

- -

1. What does being relevant mean to you?

   _____

   _____

   _____

   _____

   _____

   _____

   _____

   _____

2. What is the first step you need to take to become more relevant to your buyers?

   _____

   _____

   _____

   _____

   _____

   _____

   _____

   _____

3. Think of an example of a relevant salesperson you've encountered recently. What did he/she say or do that made you feel like the conversation was relevant to you?

_____

_____

_____

_____

_____

_____

_____

_____

4. What is stopping you from becoming more relevant with your buyers?

_____

_____

_____

_____

_____

_____

_____

_____

5. What does a relevant conversation look like with your buyers and how do you know if you've achieved it?

_____

_____

_____

_____

_____

_____

_____

_____

in·sight·ful

having or showing an accurate and deep understanding;
perceptive

Do you know the difference between providing information and providing insight?

I WAS SITTING IN A board meeting for the National Sales and Marketing Council in Washington, DC, when I received a text from my husband with a photo of my two-year-old son in what appeared to be a skydiving flight suit. The photo had no explanation. I panicked! I texted back something I cannot repeat here and demanded an explanation. Why was I so panicked? Here's the rest of the story...

My husband and son were with me that day in Washington, DC, sightseeing while I attended board meetings. As we got dressed for the day to go our separate ways, my husband said, "Guess what? I found an indoor skydiving attraction we can go to today!" While indoor skydiving sounds fun, I reminded my husband that our son was only two years old and told him under no circumstance was he to take our son indoor skydiving. Thus, you can imagine my surprise, fear, and frustration when I received a text of our son wearing what appeared to be a flight suit.

As it turned out, my husband had not taken our two-year-old son indoor skydiving. The full context of the photo was that they were at the Smithsonian National Air and Space Museum when my son had a potty training accident. Our backpack did not have an extra set of clothes in it, so my husband did what any great father would do. He took him to the gift shop at the museum and bought him new clothes. The only clothing item in a toddler size for sale in the gift shop was an astronaut flight suit. Now when I see the photo, I chuckle to myself at the whole episode, and it serves as a reminder not to jump to conclusions until I have the full story.

The second trait of a FANtastic salesperson is the ability to be insightful. We have already established in Chapter One that the internet-empowered buyer has unlimited amounts of information, data, facts, and figures at their fingertips. But what they lack and need from a salesperson is insight to help them organize, prioritize, and analyze the information. Insight gives the information context. Just like in the story above, information without context is meaningless.

Context is the background information that gives content meaning. Context explains *why* information is important, *why* it matters. It also helps someone know which pieces of information to pay attention to and which pieces can be ignored or discarded. Ultimately, context helps buyers make decisions and eliminate other choices.

When you provide a buyer with the benefit of your professional insight, you provide the framework they need to make a buying decision. The framework includes:

- How your product functions on a day-to-day basis.
- Why the features of your product matter.
- How your product compares to the competition.
- Why your product is better.
- Why the buyer needs your product.
- Why the buyer needs to purchase sooner rather than later.
- What other factors the buyer should consider based on your experience.

Too often salespeople are guilty of a data dump approach to selling. They rattle off the features of their product and service and assume the buyer understands *why* those features matter. As we discussed in Chapter One, the data dump is a major turn-off to the internet-empowered buyer, because it does not acknowledge the depth of the relationship already formed in the mind of the buyer. But that isn't the only problem with it; the data dump also stops short of moving the buyer from prospect to purchaser. If all you provide is a data dump of features, specs, and pricing, you are nothing more than an order taker. Taking orders is not selling. Order takers allow the buyer to make decisions on their own timetable. **FANtastic Selling means you are in the timeline acceleration business.** Closing a sale isn't enough to be a FANtastic salesperson if the buyer buys on *their* timeframe. Being FANtastic means you build urgency, excitement, and desire for the buyer to purchase sooner rather than later.

EXCEL OR EXTINCT—YOU DECIDE

Sales For Life recently published an infographic titled *The Rise of the Modern Salesperson* based on research from Forrester, Sales for Life, and SAP. The research indicates there are four major sales archetypes and only one of them will survive and thrive as buyers become more informed and artificial intelligence and automation increasingly replace salespeople.

- **Order Takers**—Extinct! Expect a 33% job loss or 550,000 out of 1.6 million jobs. These positions will be replaced by self-service portals, e.g., self-checkout at the grocery.

- **Explainers**—Extinct! Expect a 15% job loss or 150,000 out of 9,000,000 jobs. These positions will be replaced due to streamlined procurement procedures that require less explanation.

- **Navigators**—Extinct! Expect 25% job loss or 400,000 out of 1.5 million jobs. Websites, social media, videos, and virtual-reality tools will replace the need for salespeople who simply convey information.

- **Consultants**—Thriving! Expect a 10% job gain, 550,000 jobs and growing.

Which archetype best describes your approach to sales? We all like to think of ourselves as professional salespeople who fall into the consultant and trusted advisor category. But you know from your own personal shopping experiences, not every salesperson rises to that level. Take a hard look at your selling style and be honest with yourself moving forward. Where do you need to improve to become less of an order taker and more of a consultant? One skill that will certainly catapult you to consultant-level selling is your ability to put your product, features, and benefits into context for the buyer.

CONTEXT CREATES DISTINCTION

One of the most important aspects of creating context is to distinguish your product or service from the competition. You must help the buyer understand why your product is unique and how that matters to them (all without bashing the competition, which is highly unprofessional). Lazy salespeople rely on pricing, discounts, and incentives to establish differentiation. Without those, they can't close the sale. FANtastic Selling requires that you understand how to sell your product or service even when your prices aren't the lowest and/or when you have no discount to offer. From my experience, there are six categories of distinction that you can utilize to put your product, your company, and your personal brand into context.

1. **Price**—Brands that differentiate on price compete either as the low-cost leader or as the premium price leader. For example, McDonald's, Walmart, and IKEA are examples of low-cost leaders. Their goal is to be the lowest price in the category. In contrast, Mercedes-Benz, Tiffany & Co., and The Ritz-Carlton are the premium price leaders in their categories. Most salespeople, particularly order takers, rely solely or too heavily on price to create context and distinction. This is a dangerous habit because if/when your product is no longer the low-price leader, order takers do not know how to create context and give insight on any other attribute. If you were to remove all discussions of price from your sales pitch, how well could you create differentiation?

2. **Process**—Brands that differentiate on process stand out by doing business differently than the competition. Uber, FedEx, and CarMax are examples of companies that disrupted how business is done and reinvented the process of arranging transportation, sending packages, and buying used cars. Process is a powerful way to create distinction and can be a game changer for a salesperson. The challenge with process as a differentiator is that it may require the support of the entire organization and involve aspects of the business that are beyond the salesperson's control. If your company is innovative and truly doing business differently than the competition, then process is a FANtastic way to put your product into context.

3. **Product**—Extraordinary, groundbreaking, category-of-one products like the Apple iPod and the Dyson Ball vacuum cleaner can certainly differentiate a brand. When Apple unveiled the iPod it was a game changer because it created an entirely new product category. On a scale of 1 to 10, how unique is your product? For product differentiation to be effective, you need to be at a 9 or 10. As with price differentiation, salespeople can rely too heavily on product differentiation. If your product is not truly unique, trying to position it that way will damage your credibility with the internet-empowered buyer. We will talk about trust and credibility in detail in a later chapter. For now, suffice it to say that the one thing you cannot afford is for your fans to feel like they can't trust you. Be honest with yourself about your product. If it isn't a "unicorn of uniqueness" in your industry, learn how to create context and differentiation with one of the other five options listed here.

4. **People**—Southwest Airlines, Nordstrom, and Disney are FANtastic examples of companies that differentiate based on customer experience delivered by employees empowered to go the extra mile. While these companies differentiate themselves in other categories, ranging from price to product, they also rely on their employees—their team members—to create differentiation and context with simple interactions that exceed expectations on a daily basis. **Unlike product, price or process differentiation, this category of differentiation is completely within your control and is your best**

option to create context. Remember that buyers buy YOU first. Before they buy into your product and your company, they buy into you. Your level of service before, during, and after the sale helps to either re-sell you or un-sell you. How you conduct yourself can be the ultimate differentiator.

5. **Promotion**—Some brands differentiate based on the strength of their marketing campaigns. Progressive Insurance became a household name because of their television commercials featuring Flo the Progressive Girl. Other examples include Doritos, Bud Light, and Old Spice whose clever, offbeat, Super Bowl commercials differentiate them from the competition. While the average salesperson does not have input on corporate marketing campaigns, your personal brand and personal marketing efforts can absolutely be a promotion differentiator. In the age of social media marketing, you don't need a Super Bowl commercial to be memorable and stand out. We will talk about social selling in greater detail in a later chapter.

6. **Purpose**—For mission-driven brands, purpose is an excellent way to differentiate. Lush Cosmetics, TOMS, and Whole Foods are perfect examples of brands that differentiate based on a bigger purpose or mission. This mission resonates with their fans and keeps them engaged. Even if your company does not have a stated mission, you can make purpose part of your personal brand. If you have a passion for selling, a passion for your product, and a passion for helping your

buyers, then you have a purpose. You have a mission. That mission can shine through in every conversation and action you take throughout the sales process. Your passion and purpose is a FANtastic differentiator.

THREE EASY WAYS TO ESTABLISH CONTEXT

So how do you establish context in a sales conversation? Statements like "let me put that into context for you", "to put that information into context", or "that information is out of context" may be perceived as condescending by the buyer. The following three phrases allow you to add context to a conversation without the risk of sounding like a know-it-all. Start using these regularly and watch your closing rate dramatically improve.

So What?—The next time you start describing a feature of your product or service to a buyer, think to yourself, *so what?* The answer to *so what* is the context. Let me give you a real life example of how this technique works. I recently purchased a new carry-on piece of luggage from a FANtastic salesperson. She was pleasant, friendly, and most importantly, she helped me understand how the suitcase would work for me in real life and solve my stated frustrations. I narrowed down the options to two and the one I ultimately selected was twice as expensive as the other option. I'm totally satisfied with it and absolutely made the right choice. The following list is a small selection of the features and *so whats* she helped me understand about the Briggs and Riley™ Domestic Carry-On Expandable Spinner suitcase priced at $499.

- **The luggage features four wheels instead of two.** *So what?* The four wheels allow you to spin the luggage sideways to fit through tight spaces like the airplane aisle with ease. *So what?* This allows you to roll the suitcase down the aisle instead of carrying it sideways which may be partially responsible for your neck, shoulder, and back pain.

- **The back wheels of the suitcase are slightly larger than the front wheels.** *So what?* The larger back wheels prevent the suitcase from tipping forward when a heavy backpack is placed on top. *So what?* That means you can let go of the suitcase to pay for an order in a crowded airport food court without causing a domino effect of falling suitcases.

- **The suitcase features CX technology that allows you to pack 33% more and compress the suitcase back down to the original size.** *So what?* You can fit that extra pair of high heels shoes that you desperately want to take and you don't need to check a bag! *So what?* By carrying-on you save time and money, you are happier, and more fashionable while you wow your audience with not one, but two pairs of FANtastic high heels!

You might notice that the more you ask the *so what* question, the deeper you drill into the context and the more specific the context becomes. This is what your fans need from you. They need details and specifics. They need to understand why this product or service will make a difference to them in a real way.

To learn how to do the *so what* method of providing context, take out a piece of paper and draw a T on it. Label the left column "Feature" and label the right column "So What?" List at least 20 features of your product and service in the left column and in the right column answer the *so what* question. Be as specific as possible. You may have multiple *so what* answers per feature. That's awesome. You can select which one to give the buyer based on your discovery of what is relevant to them. You can do this exercise solo or with a partner or team. The more people who participate in the exercise the greater variety of answers you can develop.

Why?—If the *so what* method does not resonate with you, another way to provide context is to explain *why* a feature or benefit is important. While the *so what* question is a question you think to yourself and answer out loud, the *why* method is something you ask and answer out loud. The key to the why method is to use it consistently. From this moment forward, never again state a feature without concluding the sentence with *why* this matters or *why* that will help you. **A feature statement without a *why* at the end is an incomplete sentence.**

For example, let's pretend for a moment you are selling new construction homes and the model home you are demonstrating to the buyer has a master bedroom on the main floor. *Why* does a first-floor master bedroom matter? *Why* is it a benefit? *Why* will the buyer prefer a master bedroom on the main floor after they move in?

- **Increased resale value**—Master bedrooms on the main floor resell faster and for a higher price than second-story master bedrooms.

- **Convenience**—You have access to the kitchen for late-night snacks, as well as ease of putting away laundry, dry cleaning and other miscellaneous items as you bring them into the house.

- **Safety**—For aging seniors, climbing stairs can become difficult and a safety hazard.

- **Separation**—For households with young adults or frequent guests, it is nice to have separation and a quiet space away from loud music or video games.

As with the *so what* exercise, take time to plan out your *whys* before you insert them into your next pitch. Write down a list of *whys* for each feature of your product and service and you will be armed with a powerful list to create context.

Because—Similar to the *why* method, *because* is a way to complete a feature statement in a way that adds context to the conversation. When you add *because* to the sentence, you are giving the buyer a reason to purchase the product. Our minds are hardwired to seek reason, to understand why something is the way it is, why it matters, why it exists. The *because* method allows you to

explain why your company, your product, or you the salesperson does things a certain way. The *because* method works like this:

- I am going to ask you a series of questions, not to be nosy or annoying, but *because* I want to narrow down your options as quickly as possible and show you just the right option for your needs.

- I am sharing this story with you *because* it demonstrates how others have used our product successfully.

- We are reviewing these options *because* it will give you an excellent overview of what we offer.

- We offer a lifetime guarantee on our product *because* 99% of our buyers are completely satisfied and we are confident you will be too.

Whether you use the *so what, why* or *because* method for providing context, it is imperative that you start providing insight and not just information. Elevate the sales conversation from a data dump to a series of professional recommendations based on your expertise and watch your sales soar.

FORMULATE YOUR GAME PLAN

Five FANtastic Questions to Help You Become More Insightful

----

1. What does being an insightful salesperson mean to you?

_____

_____

_____

_____

_____

_____

_____

_____

2. How do you normally communicate context? What does that sound like?

_____

_____

_____

_____

_____

_____

_____

_____

3. Which of the six categories of distinction—Price, Product, Process, People, Promotion and/or Purpose—apply to your product? Your company? To you personally?

_____

_____

_____

_____

_____

_____

_____

_____

4. Which of the context clues are you currently using (*So What, Why, Because*)? Which one(s) do you want to start using that you are not using now?

_____

_____

_____

_____

_____

_____

_____

_____

5. What does an insightful conversation look like with your buyers and how do you know if you've achieved it?

_____

_____

_____

_____

_____

_____

_____

_____

_____

in·quis·i·tive

curious or inquiring

Are you insanely, insatiably, innately
curious about your fans?

DO YOU REMEMBER WHEN FLAT screen televisions first became available? My husband suggested we purchase a flat screen television for a joint Christmas gift that year and I agreed. How I ended up with a new couch, new coffee table, new end tables, and a new console table for Christmas that year, well, here's the rest of the story....

I agreed to a new flat screen television for Christmas as our joint gift to each other because I was aware of several important facts. First, the current entertainment armoire concealing the television in the family room was not designed for the new flat screen televisions. It would need to be replaced with a console table that the new TV either hung above on sat upon. Second, our current coffee table and end tables were dated and I knew finding something to match or complement them was going to be impossible. Third, the couch had seen better days, with fraying fabric and lumpy, unsupportive cushions. Thinking ahead, I understood the new television was going to start a chain reaction in our family room that would lead to an entire—and much needed—room makeover.

We went shopping for the new furniture and found ourselves frustrated and discouraged. Greeted by order taker after order taker, the salespeople predictability asked "how can I help you" to which we replied "just looking" and then they proceeded to point us in the direction of the family room furniture with no further explanation or discovery. The ironic thing is we weren't just looking. We were there to buy. Yet by opening with a cliché question, the salespeople triggered our own cliché auto-response answer, and the conversation was over before it even started. After three disappointing experiences, we were greeted at the fourth store by an enthusiastic, friendly, inquisitive salesperson named April Orlando. I know this because she introduced herself by name and asked our names. I knew immediately from her greeting that we had finally met a professional, relevant, insightful salesperson who could help us purchase furniture that we both liked and could afford. April asked permission to ask a few questions to help narrow down the options.

- What type of fabric do you prefer for the couch?
- What is the size of the room?

- How large is the television?
- Do you prefer glass or wood for the coffee table, end tables, and console table?
- How many people typically need seating in your family room?
- Are you thinking sofa and loveseat or sectional?
- Do you need a sleeper sofa?
- Do you like to sit with your feet up?
- Do you need storage in the coffee table or end tables?
- Will the new television sit on or hang above the console table?
- Do you need storage in the console table for equipment, cords, and/or DVDs?

She must have asked us 25 questions, but it wasn't annoying. It wasn't a turn off. She came across as genuinely curious about our design tastes, functionality needs, and lifestyle. We eagerly answered all of her questions and then she guided us to three options, all of which met all or most of the criteria established through her insightful questions. We easily selected the furniture from options she presented and she closed us with the promise of delivery before the holiday. We finalized the order on the spot and on Christmas day we thoroughly enjoyed watching "our" Christmas present in the newly made over family room.

The third undeniable trait of a FANtastic, rock-star, top-producing, quota-busting salesperson is to be inquisitive. FANtastic salespeople think like the iconic slogan for The National Enquirer supermarket tabloid, *enquiring minds want to know*. FANtastic salespeople are genuinely curious about people and can't get wait to get to know them better.

How inquisitive are you? Think back to your most recent sales conversation. What was your ratio of questions versus statements? What was the ratio of how much you talked versus how much the buyer talked? Inquisitive salespeople talk less than the buyer talks. They know how to ask just the right question for the situation and then let the buyer do all the talking.

Many years ago, when I was selling internet advertising during the dot-com boom, I learned the art of asking questions from a sales manager who was a master at it. When he accompanied me to sales appointments, he would kick me under the table if I was talking too much and not asking enough questions. If we were doing a virtual presentation via conference call, he would text me if I needed to stop talking and give the buyer a chance to respond. We would debrief the sales call over coffee or lunch afterwards and practice the questions I should ask next time. His focus on asking questions and tailoring the presentation to the buyer's answers changed the trajectory of my career. There is no question I am a better presenter, facilitator, and salesperson because of his training. I hope this chapter in the book can do the same for you.

THE MORE QUESTIONS THE BETTER

The concept of asking questions and the need for discovery in a sales conversation certainly isn't groundbreaking. You've probably read countless articles, blogs, and books about the art of discovery. You've probably attended seminars and boot camps just on this one topic alone. Yet, I would be willing to bet you one month's commission that if you were mystery shopped right now, the mystery shop would reveal that you don't ask enough questions. It would probably reveal that despite your best efforts, you talk too much and don't allow the buyer to talk enough. It is a common mistake that even the most seasoned salespeople make despite repeated training and education. Why do we struggle with it so much?

First, salespeople love to talk! The typical salesperson is an extrovert who seeks attention and loves to talk more than they love to listen. Second, salespeople are reluctant to ask a lot of questions out of fear they won't be able to answer the questions or because they fear the answers will kill the sale. Third, many salespeople have developed bad habits. They have been selling the same way for a long time and have lost touch with their buyer's needs and wants. Finally, many salespeople are uncomfortable with the silence that comes after you ask a question while the buyer is considering their answer. The silence can be deafening and awkward, and salespeople tend to fill the vacuum with more talking. I challenge you to start paying attention to your sales conversations. Be brutally honest with yourself. My experience says you could easily double or triple the number of questions you ask throughout the sales presentation and it still would not be too much.

The key to being inquisitive is to gain permission to ask the questions. Phrases like "may I ask you a few questions so I can tailor my presentation to your needs" or "I would like to ask you a few questions to narrow down your options" will help you ask a number of questions without coming across like a prosecutor badgering a witness.

Your tone while you are asking questions is also important. Your voice must show a genuine desire to learn more about the other person. Strike an upbeat, enthusiastic, friendly, and approachable tone. Make eye contact and listen with your ears and your eyes while the buyer answers. This lets them know you value their answer. If you interrupt the buyer's answer with another question, then it comes across like you don't really care about getting an answer and that you are simply asking questions because you are required to do so.

Lastly, you must be able to tailor your presentation based on the answers to your questions. We've all sat through sales pitches where the salesperson asked questions and then proceeded with a pre-written script and 50 PowerPoint slides that did nothing to address our answers. If you ignore the answers and proceed with sales as usual, asking questions will backfire. You will not seem trustworthy and authentic, and the buyer is sure to mentally check out until the conversation is over.

DISCOVERY #1—WHERE ARE YOU IN THE BUYING JOURNEY?

We've all been trained on the standard who, what, where, when, how and why questions to ask in sales. We've been trained to ask what is the buying timeframe and who is the decision maker. Now I want to give you something new and fresh that perhaps you haven't considered to help you avoid questions that are useless or even damaging. We are going to discuss three discovery opportunities that go beyond the cliché and trite questions that don't encourage buyers to give you an insightful answer. As I shared in my personal story at the beginning of the chapter, questions like "how can I help you" and "what brings you out today" will result in an auto-response answer from the buyer that does nothing to advance the conversation and may stop it before it even starts. If you want to engage with your buyers in a meaningful dialogue, set more second appointments, and close more sales, you must stop asking bad questions!

The first discovery you must make is which stage of the buying journey they are in. In the companion title to this book, *FANtastic Marketing*, I go into great detail about the phases of the buyer's journey. Even if you aren't responsible for marketing, I encourage you to read that book. There are many crossover concepts that salespeople can learn, including the buyer's journey. Likewise, I encourage marketing professionals to read this book. Marketing and sales are two sides of the same coin and that's exactly why I chose to write both books.

Without repeating too much of the information in *FANtastic Marketing*, there are three phases to the buyer's journey: 1) Awareness, 2) Consideration, and 3) Decision. In the Awareness phase the buyer is just becoming aware of potential dissatisfaction with their current solution and is determining whether they want to take further action. In the Consideration phase, the buyer has committed to making a change and is reviewing options. In the Decision phase, the buyer has narrowed down the options and is deciding which one to select.

Why does the phase of the buying journey matter to you? Well, this is your first clue on how to tailor your presentation to their needs. A buyer in the Awareness phase needs different types of information than a buyer in the Consideration or Decision phases. Also, the phase of the buying journey reveals how long the buyer has been shopping for solutions and how close they are to making a decision. Finally, the phase of the buying journey reveals the level of interest and investment of the buyer to help you prioritize your time.

In my sales training seminars and keynotes, I always ask this question: "How do you know what phase of the buying journey the buyer is in?" And I always get the same answer: "You ask them questions!" Of course. Asking questions is a very important way to determine the phase of the buying journey. The answer I am looking for and rarely ever hear from the audience is this: *You can tell the phase of the buying journey by the questions the buyers ask you.*

Have you ever considered that the questions the buyer asks you are clear signals of their phase in the buying journey? We so often fail to listen to the whole question because we want to appear smart, knowledgeable, and savvy. We forget to listen and consider what the question means about the buyer's process. From now on, start listening to your buyer's questions, not only to answer them, but to see what they reveal about the buyer's journey.

Let's say, for example, you are an advertising agency that provides marketing for small businesses. Where in the buyer's journey do these questions from potential clients fall?

- Do you provide marketing services for insurance agencies? What types of services do you offer?
- Do you build websites in Wordpress? What is your pricing for a Wordpress website and what are the monthly hosting fees?
- If we move forward with your proposal, what are the next steps and how do we get started?

If you guessed Awareness, Consideration, and Decision in that order, then you guessed correctly. Awareness questions tend to be broad questions that help the buyer establish a big-picture sense of your products and services. Consideration questions are more specific and ask you to detail the features and benefits of your products. Decision questions compare you to others and ask you to draw a sharp contrast between options. As you answer these questions, don't forget to use the *So What, Why,* and *Because* methods of establishing context that we discussed in the last chapter.

DISCOVERY #2—WHAT IS THE PURPOSE OF THIS CONVERSATION?

I had been shopping at the mall for three hours. Not the leisurely strolling, browsing, and chatting with a girlfriend type of shopping. This was the on a deadline, leaving tomorrow, and want a new outfit to speak in front of 1,000 people type of shopping. I was discouraged, hot, and thirsty. I had found nothing that fit well and gave me the confidence I was looking for. My very last stop was White House Black Market, a popular, upscale women's clothing store located in most malls. As I walked in, I was greeted by Jessica, who introduced herself as the store sales manager and asked me for my name. From reading the previous section, you know how I feel about trite, boilerplate greetings, so this shopping experience was already off to a good start!

That's when Jessica slayed me with a killer opening question that changed the way I open all of my sales conservations. She asked, "what's the mission today?" Jessica was the first one in three hours of shopping to ask, in a unique, interesting way, *why* I was shopping. All of the other retail salespeople had either failed to ask the purpose of my visit, or had asked a stale question such as "looking for something special" which automatically triggers most buyer's auto-response answer of "just browsing." The "what's the mission today" question stopped me in my tracks. I couldn't blow her off and tell her I was just looking. It made me want to answer her. It signaled to me that she was professional, advanced, and possessed the skills to help me.

I told her what I was looking for and that's when she slayed me a second time. She replied with "why don't you take a break and have a seat in our dressing room. I will pull several options for you to try on and we'll see what works." At that moment, I knew I was about to spend a lot of money!!! Jessica pulled three complete outfits, including shoes and jewelry. All three met my criteria perfectly and I had the luxury of deciding which one was more my personal taste. I selected one entire outfit and— several hundred dollars later—I was completely satisfied with my purchase. I went on to the speaking event and felt confident and appropriately dressed for the occasion.

Lesson number one from this story: replace your boring, obvious, auto-response questions with new, fresh questions that make the buyer want to answer you. Lesson number two: establish up front what the buyer wants to get out of the conversation. You can ask questions like "what's the agenda today" or "what are you hoping to get out of this meeting?" Use your own words and your own style, just don't fail to establish the purpose of the conversation. Periodically throughout the conversation, stop and check-in to make sure you are meeting the stated objective. We'll talk more about checking in in a later chapter.

DISCOVERY #3—WHAT INFORMATION DO YOU ALREADY KNOW?

In Chapter One, we talked about the importance of respecting the buyer's research and knowledge during your initial sales conversation. The only way to accomplish that is to find out what information is known already. How will you do that? Ask them! The following questions will help you determine how much the buyer knows, what they know about your company or product, and what information they are still lacking:

- Have you visited our website?
- (If yes) What did you see that you liked?
- What do you know about our company?
- Are you familiar with our services?
- Are you familiar with this product?
- What solutions have you researched so far?
- What information are you looking to gain today?
- Do you know anyone that is already using our product(s)?
- What prompted you to call/email/text/visit me today?

Most books and educational programs on sales skip these questions and advise you to go straight into asking questions like "tell me about your business" and "what current frustrations are you experiencing?" These are good questions if you are in a cold-calling or first-appointment scenario where you initiated the meeting. However, in today's global economy where we are all interconnected by social media, most of your sales conversations are going to happen because the buyer already knows something about you. Perhaps you connected on LinkedIn and you followed up with a request for coffee to get to know each other better. Or perhaps the buyer submitted an email or live chat request via your website for more information. They may have called in to a sales toll-free number and been directed to your voicemail. No matter how you connect, your easiest, quickest, and most profitable sales happen when the buyer comes to you. If this isn't happening, keep reading (and buy a copy of *FANtastic Marketing*).

The days of cold calling as an effective method to win new sales is over. I'm not saying you won't get lucky on occasion with a cold call, but it is not a sustainable way of generating new business. In today's voicemail, caller ID, spam filter world, we simply do not respond to cold calls. Our preferred method of handling them is to ignore, delete, and mark as junk. To make sales today, you must establish yourself as an expert, consultant, and trusted advisor who solves problems. Your sphere of influence must be wide and deep in your industry. When people think of your name, they should automatically think *he/she solves* _____ *(fill in the blank with the problem you solve)*.

Once you've achieved this status, the next step is to be insanely, insatiably, innately curious about the buyer, their business, what they know about you, their agenda for the meeting, and where they are in the buying journey.

FORMULATE YOUR GAME PLAN

Five FANtastic Questions to Help You Become More Inquisitive

----

1. What does being an inquisitive salesperson mean to you?

_____

_____

_____

_____

_____

_____

_____

_____

2. What is the difference between inquisitive and nosy? How do
you strike a balance?

_____

_____

_____

_____

_____

_____

_____

_____

3. List one question you frequently are asked in each phase of the buying journey.

Awareness _____

_____

_____

Consideration _____

_____

_____

Decision _____

_____

_____

4. Approximately how many questions do you ask during a typical sales conversation? What steps do you need to take to ask more questions?

_____

_____

_____

_____

_____

_____

_____

_____

_____

5. What is your favorite question that guarantees a response nearly every time you ask it? Share it with me at Meredith@CreatingWOW.com.

_____

_____

_____

_____

_____

_____

_____

_____

en·gag·ing

very attractive or pleasing in a way that holds your attention

---

What do Coca-Cola®, Starbucks®, and Burger King® have in common besides tasty beverages?

I SPENT THE SUMMER OF 2014 looking through displays of Coca-Cola trying to find one with my son's name on it. From Walgreens to Target to Kroger, everywhere we went that had a Coke display, he insisted we stop and search through hundreds of Coke cans and bottles. We never did find one that said "Brady" on it much to the dismay of my son. Finally, out of frustration, he said to me, "Mommy, why don't you just call Coke and tell them to make one with my name on it!" Here's the rest of the story...

The "Share a Coke" campaign launched in the summer of 2014 and it was one of the most successful marketing campaigns ever produced by Coca-Cola. In case you missed it, Coke replaced its own iconic logo on the packaging of Coke, Diet Coke, and Coke Zero with popular consumer first names like John and Susan, popular nicknames like "Mom" and "Best Friend," and even adjectives like "Super Star" and "Hero". The 2014 campaign resulted in a 2% increase in soft-drink sales, increasing consumption from 1.7 billion to 1.9 billion servings per day, making #shareacoke a number-one global-trending topic on social media.[5] For the first time in ten years, Coca-Cola sales increased as a result of the campaign.[6] It was so successful that Coke ran the campaign again in 2015 and 2016 with more names, more packages, and more ways to share. By 2015, many more names were included in the campaign and you didn't have to search randomly for your name on bottles in displays. You could search the ShareaCoke. com website to see if your name was included in the campaign. If your name was not included, no worries; you could order either an individual glass bottle or a case of bottles with any name.

As Coca-Cola itself admitted, for teens and millennials, personalization is not just a fad but is, in fact, a way of life. These consumers place high value on self-expression, individual storytelling and staying connected with friends. The "Share a Coke" campaign gives the ability to do all of these things while promoting the Coca-Cola brand.

For example, when a consumer shares a name-branded Coke bottle with her mother, she feels as if she is honoring her mother rather than promoting the Coke brand itself. Further, by taking and sharing photos of these moments with the #ShareaCoke hashtag, consumers drive more personal online media content that increases shareability.

While there were 250 common names that could have been used, not everyone's name is common, which could have decreased the personalization of the campaign. Knowing this, Coca-Cola created a 500-stop, cross-country "Share a Coke" tour that allowed fans to customize a Coca-Cola mini can for themselves and a second one for someone special. The company tour also provided alternative options with nicknames such as "bestie," "star" or "BFF." This added an additional personal touch for consumers.[7]

The Share a Coke campaign was so effective because it made the experience of drinking and sharing a Coke about the fans. The campaign tapped into our deep desire and appreciation for personalization. The more personalized the experience, the more connected we feel to it.

The fourth undeniable trait of a rock-star, top-producing, quota-busting, FANtastic salesperson is the ability to be engaging. Being engaging is about getting and keeping your fans' attention. Getting and keeping attention is a true challenge for a salesperson. Think about how many of your emails and voicemails receive no response. During the last sales presentation you had with one of your fans, how many times did he or she stop to check their phone, take a call, or respond to an email/text while you were talking? The overall lack of response from our fans, and their distracted nature, is one of the reasons I feel it is important to remind you that they are indeed fans of your product, service, brand, or of you personally or they would not start a conversation with you. I understand that based on their behavior it would be easy for you to start assuming they aren't all that interested, that you are dealing with mostly "tire kickers" who are more interested in the free cookie or beverage offered during the conversation than purchasing something from you. The fact is they are still interested and their online shopping and researching habits prove it. Most buyers are deep into the buying process before they engage with a salesperson the first time. So it's not a lack of interest that causes them to ignore you and be unresponsive. It is because we have popcorn brain!

> *Researcher David Levy calls this phenomenon popcorn brain, defined as a brain so accustomed to the constant stimulation of electronic multitasking that its owner soon becomes unfit for life offline, where events transpire at a much slower pace. In this day and age, we all suffer from a little bit of popcorn brain. Today, this tendency to popcorn brain isn't a personality flaw, but rather a biological imperative. Why? It's because the human brain craves stimulation and new information.*
>
> *Your challenge is to figure out how to leverage the popcorn brain phenomena into a dynamic which will earn new customers and clients. Let's face it: your fans are distracted and overwhelmed. This means you must work extra hard to get and keep their attention.*[8]

The remedy for popcorn brain is being engaging. What is engaging to today's popcorn-brain, media-multitasking, selfie-obsessed fan? Personalization. As the Share a Coke campaign proved, when you make your marketing about the fans, they perk up, pay attention, focus, participate, and most importantly, they buy. The same exact principle is true for sales. **The number one reason your emails, text messages, and phone calls are ignored or deleted is because the message is about you and not about them.** The reason they drift off during your presentations and start surfing on their smartphone is because they perceive that the information isn't relevant to their needs or personalized to their situation.

PERSONALIZATION IS EXPECTED

For my son's second birthday he received a Dora the Explorer hardback book titled *Brady and Dora Go on an Adventure*. The book features my son's face superimposed on a little boy character in the book and the story uses his name throughout. No wonder he was so frustrated when he couldn't find a Coke bottle with his name on it. From the age of two he has been trained to expect the highest levels of personalization. Turns out the 1974 Burger King slogan "Have It Your Way" was way ahead of its time!

My son isn't alone with his personalization expectations. While he isn't old enough to be a purchasing consumer yet, the generation before him, the millennials, certainly are, and they value an authentic experience and personalized products/services over everything else.

Millennial customers are clearly an enormous commercial force to be reckoned with, commanding both trendsetting power and tremendous spending power as well. And this millennial spending power encompasses both their own personal spending (it's estimated they'll be spending $200 billion annually by 2017 and $10 trillion over their lifetimes as consumers, in the U.S. alone) and the purse strings that millennials are beginning to control at the companies where they work, as millennials move into positions in industry with significant spending power.

There are about 80 million millennials (born 1980-2000) in the U.S. alone; to put it another way, they make up some 25% of the U.S. population—and thanks to immigration, they're a generation that is actually increasing in size. And they're a highly influential population that influences the buying decisions of other demographic cohorts. Which means it's time to put away any residual snark and learn to understand these youthful customers if you're going to be able to create a millennial-friendly sales, customer experience and customer service approach.[9]

The best proof for the demand and expectation of personalization is our obsession with Starbucks Coffee. Did you know there are 87,000 possible Starbucks drink combinations?[10] If you've ever stood behind someone at a Starbucks with an impossibly complicated drink order, you know it all too well! From our coffee to our tennis shoes, our cars to our home décor, nearly everything for sale today to consumers can be personalized. And if it can't, the product doesn't last very long.

PERSONALIZATION IS NOT FOR THE FAINT OF HEART

Personalizing the sales experience makes it more engaging. Most salespeople do not have control over product development, so the degree the actual product or service can be personalized isn't something they can influence. However, to personalize the sales experience, your first task is to break the buyer's journey into steps and look for opportunities to make the experience more engaging at each step. There are many articles, blogs, videos, and infographics available online about the buyer's journey. A quick Google search will provide you with a wide variety of opinions on how many phases are in the buyer's journey and what to name each one. Ultimately, what is important is that you can define and articulate your fan's buying journey. What are the typical steps to purchasing your product or service? Review your last 25 sales. What do those buyers have in common with regard to their process from becoming aware of a need to deciding your solution was the right one for them?

In Chapter Three we discussed the importance of asking questions to determine what phase of the buying journey the fan is in when they reach out to you for more information. For the purpose of that discussion and this one, I've defined the buyer's journey with the following three phases: 1) Awareness, 2) Consideration, and 3) Decision. Personalization of the Awareness phase will largely happen via your marketing. That is why I spent so much time discussing this topic in *FANtastic Marketing*. However, once the fan reaches the Consideration and Decision phases, at some point they are going to reach out to a salesperson and that is when you must begin engaging them with a personalized, customized experience.

What does your Consideration phase typically involve? Phone call, online demo, in-person meeting or virtual meeting? Whatever the format of that encounter, personalizing the sales experience is hard work. It requires you to concentrate and pay attention. Not the *making my grocery list in my head during this meeting* type of attention but intense, focused, *I'm only thinking about you and your needs* type of attention. How present are you when you are with your customers? Are you constantly feeding your popcorn brain by checking your phone and media-multitasking while you are talking to your customers? If you are, stop. It's a bad habit we are all guilty of, but you must stop. When you are meeting with your customers, whether it's in person or virtual, make that meeting your only priority. Put your phone away. Talk less (translated—*shut up!*). Let go of your agenda and be open to the client's agenda for the meeting. Stop fake-listening and waiting for the opportunity to get your own points across.

It may be that checking your phone is not a temptation for you, but you find yourself drifting off mentally during meetings or conversations. Perhaps you are stressed out with work issues, preoccupied with personal challenges, or you are tired and not feeling well that day. If this is the case, you need to learn to stay focused and attentive even when you are having a bad day. The best way to do this is to take detailed notes. Write down everything. If you take notes electronically, close all of your apps and software on your laptop or tablet so you are not tempted to check them during the meeting. Not only will you have the best records in the room (for which your clients will love you), but you will keep your mind engaged during the entire meeting.

When you concentrate, engage, and pay attention, you will pick up on subtle and not so subtle clues about your fans' likes, dislikes, preferences, emotions, needs, and desires that you can use to personalize your proposal, presentation, and products. I am going to give you several personalization ideas and tech tools in Chapters 8 and 9 that you can use for the Consideration and Decision phases. For now, I want to focus on the issue of paying attention and concentration, because you can't personalize if you don't know your fans. And you won't know your fans if you don't pay attention.

Traditional sales education does not typically cover skills like paying attention and concentration, but in today's world it is just as important as your ability to overcome objections or to ask for the sale. As an added bonus, the people in your personal life will appreciate your renewed focus on being present in the moment, giving undivided attention, and concentrating solely on them during a conversation. Your personal relationships will be better than ever.

Personalization does not have to be complicated or expensive, but it does require thoughtfulness. The ability to remember someone's likes, favorites, and preferences, and then take action on that information in a way that is thoughtful and creative, is the pinnacle of personalization. You don't need a multi-million dollar marketing campaign like the Share a Coke campaign to make an impact. In fact, sometimes the smallest touch, consistently executed, can have the biggest impact.

For example, the next time you meet with your one of your fans, you might include thoughtful, personalized touches such as:

- Favorite beverage mentioned in a previous conversation waiting for them in the conference room or that you take with you to the meeting.
- Favorite music playing in the background of the conference room or your office.
- Card or small gift to acknowledge a recent celebration like an engagement, wedding, or birth of a child.
- Appropriate snacks based on the fan's diet, i.e. gluten-free, vegan, and/or vegetarian.

Another low-cost way to personalize the sales experience is to simply remember the name or some other detail about the people you come across while you are networking, meeting, and mingling. We've all had the situation where we have introduced ourselves repeatedly to the same person who never remembers us. I found myself in one situation where it happened so many times with the same person that out of frustration I said, "we've met several times!" It was a little awkward after that so I don't necessarily recommend that approach.

I readily admit I don't always remember someone's name, but I work hard at remembering something about them—where they work, personal hobbies or passions, or the city/event where we met each other. I find that most people have very low expectations of being remembered, and when you can recall something about them, their eyes light up and an instant connection is formed. It is hard to remember someone's name and for that reason I think many salespeople give up on remembering anything or use that as an excuse not to try. I find people are fairly forgiving the first time if you don't remember their name. We've all been there. You can make up for it if you demonstrate a glimmer of facial recognition and can associate that person with some personal fact about them. The real reason why we don't remember names isn't because we are getting old and have a faulty memory (although that is not helping the situation). After all, most of you have no problem remembering the things that are important to you—the stats of your favorite sports team or the number of black high-heel shoes in your closet. We don't remember because of a lack of concentration and not paying attention to the other person while they are talking.

Many years ago I competed in the Miss Florida Pageant, a state preliminary for the Miss America Pageant. The first year I competed in Miss Florida, I won a preliminary talent award and a community service award. As a result, the following year I was confident that I could finish in the Top Ten and perhaps even be a Top-Five finalist. But that was not what happened. I received no preliminary awards and did not place in the Top Ten finalists, much less the Top Five. I was devastated. I had essentially gone backward in the competition. When I met with my voice coach, I expected her to commiserate with me and denounce the unjust results of the evening (as I perceived them). To my surprise, she agreed with the outcome and was not complimentary of my talent performance. She said that while I had sung the Puccini aria flawlessly from a technical perspective, I had failed to connect with the audience and communicate the emotions behind the words. As hard as it was to hear, she was right. I had to be honest with myself that on that night, I was so preoccupied with my performance, how I was being perceived, and being technically correct, that I let that get in the way of being present in the moment. I didn't make it about the audience that night. I made it about me. And when I do that, or when you do that in a sales situation, your fans check out.

I don't know what keeps you from being fully present with your fans, preventing you from personalizing the experience. Maybe you don't have an issue with being distracted by your phone or getting so focused on being technically accurate that you fail to connect. Only you can determine what keeps you from being present so you can pay attention and concentrate. I hope you are taking time to do the Formulate Your Game Plan questions at the end of each chapter. For this chapter, they are specifically designed to help you uncover how you can become more engaging via personalization with your fans.

FORMULATE YOUR GAME PLAN

Five FANtastic Questions to Help You Become More Engaging

----

1. Think of an example of someone you find very engaging. It could be someone you know personally, or an athlete, celebrity, or political figure. What does that person say and/or do that you find so engaging?

    _____

    _____

    _____

    _____

    _____

    _____

    _____

2. How difficult is it for you to stay engaged and focused during conversations and meetings with your fans? Are you doing something else while the other person is talking?

    _____

    _____

    _____

    _____

    _____

    _____

    _____

 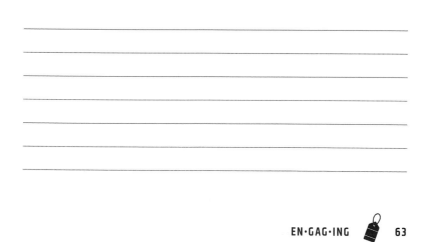

3. What's stopping you from being fully present, engaged, and paying attention during sales conversations?

---

4. Imagine for a moment you are the client. What type of personalization would be meaningful to you?

5. If you were going to coach a salesperson on being engaging, what would your number one tip be?

_____

_____

_____

_____

_____

_____

_____

_____

6. Bonus Question: List one way per phase of the Buyer's Journey that you could consistently personalize the buyer's experience.

Awareness _____

_____

_____

Consideration _____

_____

_____

Decision _____

_____

_____

 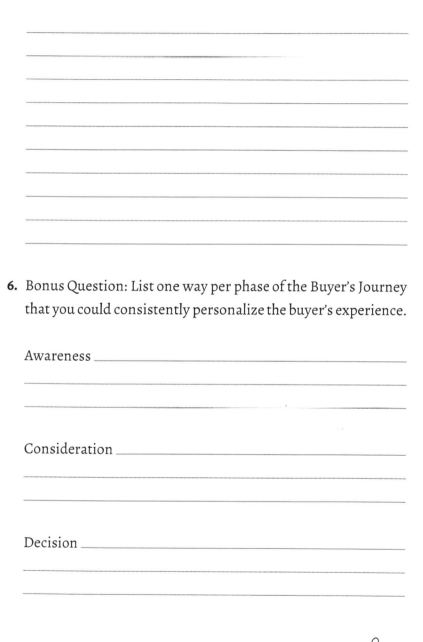

au·then·tic

real or genuine; not copied or false

Are you more focused on closing the deal or being the real deal?

I WAS SITTING IN THE hotel lobby chatting with two of my colleagues after an association board meeting. We were venting to each other about several frustrating issues regarding the association and swapping war stories. Suddenly from the corner of my eye I saw a man walking toward me with an angry expression. He stood over me and began to berate me regarding the content of our conversation. He became so animated, angry, and aggressive, the front desk clerk came over to intervene. What was he so angry about? Here's the rest of the story...

As it turns out, he was also a member of the association, although he belonged to a different local chapter. He happened to be staying at the same hotel where we were having our meeting. He was having dinner and drinks a few seats away from where we were sitting, heard parts of our conversation, and pieced together a narrative that was not accurate, was out of context, and cast us in a negative light. To make matters worse, he took what he thought he heard and posted it to the association's national Facebook page to "report" our behavior. To say it was a troubling few minutes as I tried to de-escalate the situation would be a gross understatement. My career literally flashed before my eyes. My colleagues came to my defense, but their anger was only inflaming the situation so I asked them to step away. Fortunately, after a long discussion, I was able to neutralize the situation, correct the record, and persuade him to remove the Facebook post.

Can you imagine having something you thought was said in private broadcast to the world on social media? And, that the information broadcast was not factual? The incident stayed with me for days. It shook me to the core. While I certainly wasn't my highest and best self that night, gossiping and complaining, I was doing so in private (or so I thought) with two people I trusted implicitly. I wasn't using inappropriate language or politically incorrect terminology. Yet, this other person found my behavior offensive enough to become irate and publicly post about it on social media.

Why am I sharing this very personal, embarrassing, and difficult incident with you? **This story perfectly illustrates the fifth trait of a rock-star, top-producing, quota-busting salesperson: the ability**

to be authentic and what happens in today's world when someone perceives you to be less than authentic. Authenticity is not a trait that will help you be more successful if you *happen* to possess it and can communicate it to others. It has become a business imperative. We live in a world that seeks out and craves authenticity so much so, that the moment we interpret a brand or a person's behavior as fake, we jump to conclusions and readily share our perspective on social media. If a scenario such as the one that happened to me hasn't happened to you yet, I am sad to say it probably will. We live in a world that immediately rejects anyone or anything that seems false, fake, and/or corrupt. To go a step further, we not only reject the people or things that seem fake, we publicly air those frustrations to the rest of the world, as a result of the prevalence of smartphones and social media.

WELCOME TO THE ERA OF DISTRUST

Banks that were too big to fail, failed. Political heroes on both sides of the aisle promised hope and change, and then lied, cheated, and stole from us. Sports heroes who became our cultural icons lied about using performance-enhancing drugs. Airbags that were known to be faulty were placed into cars. Perhaps most damaging to the public trust, religious leaders who had sworn to devote their lives to the church, violated our most vulnerable and precious gifts, our children, while their superiors covered up the crimes. The result is that we find ourselves in an era of distrust; a time in which we can't naively believe what others tell us. Abraham Lincoln said it best when he said, "The problem with quotes on the internet is that it is hard to verify their authenticity." Get it? Sorry for the bad joke, but I had to break up this depressing state of affairs with a little bit of humor.

So here we are living in an era of skepticism and distrust. Now add to that the rising prevalence of smartphones and social media. With two-thirds of Americans smartphone owners[11], the general public has been transformed into an army of amateur photojournalists ready and able to capture every moment of inauthentic behavior, either as a photo, audio, or video recording. What do we do with the moments we capture on our phones? Blast them out on social media of course! Social media gives us a voice. While social media has many positive applications, unfortunately it also has given rise to mob mentality where we vilify and bully others often without all the facts. Also, in a more subtle sense, social media has validated and increased our already skeptical nature because we read and see things on social media that we know to be false but are portrayed as ideal or perfect.

AUTHENTICITY IS BIG BUSINESS

Do you remember in 2014 when Hollywood actress Jennifer Lawrence tripped going up the stairs at the Academy Awards to accept her award for Best Actress? Winning an Oscar for Best Actress is the pinnacle of any movie actress's career. In the biggest moment of her career to date, she tripped and wiped out on the stairs leading up to the stage. What happened next endeared her to the public forever. Instead of pretending it didn't happen or crying from embarrassment, she made a joke and received a standing ovation! "Thank you so much! This is nuts. You guys are only standing up because I fell and you feel bad. That was embarrassing." To this day, Lawrence's candid, down-to-earth, authentic personality is what her fans love about her.

Authenticity is big business not only for Hollywood celebrities, but for brands as well. The Dove Campaign for Real Beauty is a classic marketing case study on how to tap into the desire for authenticity. It was a worldwide marketing campaign launched in 2004 by Unilever to promote Dove beauty products and the goal was to celebrate the natural beauty of "real" women.[12] The women featured in the ads were regular women in lieu of professional models and featured a wide range of ethnicities, sizes, and ages. The campaign was one of the first ad campaigns to go viral, generating media exposure estimated to be worth 30 times the paid-for media space, and it started a global conversation to widen the definition of beauty.

The desire for authenticity is so strong it's why we pay twice as much for products labeled as organic. It's why we elect political leaders who are labeled "outsiders" over "establishment" candidates who have twice the political resume and experience. It's why we cheer for the underdog in reality television competitions like *The Voice, Dancing With the Stars,* and *America's Got Talent.* We want the dog walker, the waitress, and/or the military veteran amputee to be the winner because we consider them to be "the real deal."

Reader's Digest recently announced the results of their second annual Trusted Brand Survey. More than 5,000 Americans across the country participated in the online survey, which awards the "Reader's Digest Most Trusted Brand" title to winners in 40 product categories.[13]

In today's world, trust is perhaps more important than ever, but also more elusive and fleeting. The survey found that trust continues to be a very important factor in consumer decision making, with 78 percent of this year's survey participants stating they would choose a brand that's been identified as more trustworthy than a different brand with equal quality and price.

In addition, the study reported 67 percent of U.S. adults surveyed pay more attention to trusted brands, and another 67 percent say they pay more money to support trusted brands. Furthermore, half of respondents (50 percent) said the Reader's Digest Most Trusted Brands seal would increase their likelihood of trusting that product or service.

From Southwest Airlines, to Folgers coffee, to Advil pain reliever, to Apple computers, to Dove soap, the *Reader's Digest* contest winners are also the industry leaders in every product category. **The fact of the matter is trust = sales.** While this certainly isn't a new concept—we've known for decades that we buy from people and brands that we like and trust—what is different is that our tolerance level for disingenuous, dishonest, deceitful behavior is at an all-time low. Now we have a vehicle in social media to spread our opinions quickly and powerfully.

What does this mean for you, the salesperson, the entrepreneur or the business owner? It means that competence, the act of doing your job and doing it well, is not enough for your fans. Competence is expected. Competence does not add value to your offering. It is considered the price of doing business. What matters more than competence is your credibility. Your intentions, the reason why you are in business, and how you conduct yourself with customers are as important as performing the basic functions of your job. If your fans do not believe that you are acting in their best interest, they don't care how good a job you do. The jig is up. If your company, your product, and your performance is not trustworthy, authentic, and sincere, it is only a matter of time before you will be out of business.

TRUST BREAKER #1—MAKE IT ABOUT YOU

If you have taken the time to read this book and care enough to improve your performance, chances are you are a person who values authenticity and trustworthiness. You probably consider yourself a person of integrity and high moral ethics. What you may not have considered or realized before reading this chapter is that we all have habits or subconscious actions that are trust breakers despite our best intentions. The goal of this section is to help you become more aware of these habits and perhaps even spark some awareness of other habits that are not mentioned here.

A trust breaker is a behavior that is incongruent with your words. For example, it's when you say things like "I'm not mad!" but your face is flaming red, the veins on your neck are popping out, and your fists are clenched, clearly indicating something to the contrary. If you want your fans to trust you, then your words and actions must be congruent.

The first trust breaker we will examine is when salespeople state, "Our customers are our first priority" or "This meeting is to learn all about you and your needs" and then proceed to dominate the entire conversation. When you, the salesperson, talk more than you listen, it's an immediate trust breaker. It renders your words to the contrary meaningless. Why should I believe anything else you have to say if the most basic premise of the conversation "that it's about me and my needs" isn't true? In every single chapter so far, I've discussed the need for salespeople to talk less. If I haven't convinced you by now, then perhaps the realization that you are actually damaging your credibility is what will get your attention. Yes, when you talk less, you can learn more about the buyer. Yes, when you talk less, you validate your fans, and become more engaging. Yes, when you talk less, you can pick up on clues to personalize the sales process and experience. All of this is true. But perhaps more than anything, when you talk less, your fans actually believe that you are here to serve them.

In addition to talking too much, there are other trust breakers that make it all about you and not them. Some salespeople cannot stop themselves from the "one-up" habit where no matter what the fan says they have a more impressive experience or anecdote to share. Picture this scenario: you are chatting with a fan and happen to notice they are driving a new car. The one-upper will compliment the new car, but can't stop there. They have to continue on with something like "I know how wonderful it is to have a new car; our new Porsche SUV drives like a dream." Really? Your new Porsche SUV? Was it necessary to add on that last part? No! A FANtastic salesperson stops with a genuine and sincere compliment to the fan and does not make it about herself or himself by bringing themselves into the conversation.

How about the salespeople who over-correct others during conversations? These individuals feel the need to be right or to set the record straight about the smallest of details that aren't that important. Just like talking too much and one-upping, over-correcting sends a signal that I care more about being right or maintaining my authority in the conversation than I do about the person speaking.

If you are doing any of these things, you probably are not aware of it. Most readers who take the time to learn and grow have good intentions, and I have no doubt you truly want the best for your fans. I hope by reading this chapter, you are more aware that despite your best efforts to be competent at your job, your credibility is on the line when, whether intentionally or unintentionally, your words and actions are not congruent.

TRUST BREAKER #2—DON'T EXPLAIN THE PROCESS

Have you ever been called into your boss's office for a meeting or performance review and during the conversation your boss suddenly starts taking notes? Or, how about the last time you visited the doctor or attorney, and out of the blue they furrowed their brow and started writing down notes. What is your instant reaction? Most of us want to know what they are writing and why. Our assumption is it must be bad news. Our minds go to all kinds of negative places trying to figure out what is happening.

Your fans do the same thing when you don't explain the sales and buying process to them. In order for them to trust you, they need to know why you are demonstrating a particular sample, why you are asking so many questions, why you are taking notes, and why you are calling the main office for more information.

One of my favorite rides at Walt Disney World is The Pirates of the Caribbean. Guests on the ride set sail in small motorized boats on a nine-minute journey through a series of pirate-themed vignettes while the ride's classic anthem "Yo Ho, Yo Ho (A Pirate's Life For Me)" blares in the background. (If you are familiar with the song it will be stuck in your head all day now.) There are fireworks, smoke, a sighting of Jack Sparrow, and even a little white-water drop to get your blood pumping during the ride. What fascinates me about this ride is that even though I've been on the ride dozens of times, even though I know for a fact that the boat is locked onto a motorized track, I still get a thrill of excitement from the ride every time. My senses take over; reason is suspended, and for nine minutes my inner child claps with glee. I share this with you because I believe a FANtastic sales-person is like a great ride at Disney World. You are guiding the fans through a pre-determined sales process much like a motor-ized boat locked onto a track in the Pirates of the Caribbean ride. FANtastic selling is when you do it with so much finesse, person-alization, and customization, that the fan doesn't feel the track. They feel a thrill, a moment of letting go, so much so that they can relax and trust in the process to give them the best possible solution to their needs.

In order for this to happen, you must be diligent about explaining the process and next steps throughout the conversation. Telegraph early and often, clearly and succinctly, the sales process and next steps to your fans. You can use the contextual clues *So What?*, *Why*, and *Because* discussed in Chapter Two to make the transition from step to step.

TRUST BREAKER #3—FAIL TO ASK FOR FEEDBACK

How are we doing so far? This very simple question is an excellent way to convey that you genuinely care if the conversation is meeting the fan's needs. When you stop talking long enough to check in, it signals to the fan that you are paying attention and that you care enough to make a course correction if needed. When you fail to ask for feedback, it is another way of signaling that you are more interested in your agenda than theirs. And that's a trust breaker for sure.

In addition to asking for feedback about the meeting, ask your fan's opinion about your products or services throughout the meeting. Doing so and then listening intently to the answers is a great trust builder.

- What do you like most about this? Dislike most?
- Where do you think there is room for improvement?
- How well do you envision this working for your company?
- What about it do you love? Or hate?
- What did I get wrong about your needs or challenges? Get right?
- What would you do differently if you were us?
- Is this conversation meeting your needs and expectations?

Salespeople fail to ask for feedback, just as they fail to ask questions, because they are afraid of the answers. What if the feedback is overwhelmingly negative? What if the feedback uncovers shortcomings for which there is no easy rebuttal? What if the feedback emboldens the fan to terminate the relationship or decide not to start one at all? The truth is your customer is thinking these things whether they express them to you or not, and unexpressed concerns kill sales. There is nothing you can do to save a sale when you don't know why they are no longer interested.

TRUST BREAKER #4—FAIL TO FOLLOW THROUGH

The final trust breaker in this section is the failure to follow through. Nothing says "I don't really care about you" like a failure to follow through on promises made. We frequently hear the motto "under promise and over deliver." My thinking is simple: promise and deliver. Do exactly what you say you are going to do. Nothing less. If you say you are going to call on Tuesday, call on Tuesday. If you promise more detailed answers, get the answers ASAP and follow up. If you promise a brochure will be in the mail or a link for a free trial service, then get the brochure in the mail and hit send on the email. It's really that simple. I wish I could make it more complicated. Bottom line, when you fail to follow through on a promise to a fan, it is a trust breaker. You may get a second or third chance, but eventually the chances will run out and your credibility will be irreparably damaged.

THE VELVETEEN RABBIT OF AUTHENTICITY

Before we conclude this chapter, please allow me to issue some words of caution regarding authenticity. First, authenticity in the business world must be a win-win for you and the fans. Some salespeople use authenticity as an excuse for bad behavior. Those individuals say things like "That's just who I am" or "I'm an open book; what you see is what you get" and then proceed to act in way that is hurtful to others, such as being overly blunt, talking too much, or being highly critical. If your authentic behavior is causing pain for others, straining your relationships, limiting your potential, and/or casting doubt among your fans as to your true intentions, then it is not a win-win and you need to reign in that behavior.

Second, some salespeople have no problem being so transparent and authentic that they are wide-open to the world, willingly and eagerly sharing every aspect of their life with others. Depending on your fans, this level of transparency may or may not be appropriate. In a business setting, I liken the rules for authenticity to the rules for professional dress. In a business environment, we understand a certain level of professional dress is necessary to make and to maintain a good impression. At the same time, we don't want to completely lose who we are in the process. (I once worked in sales for a hospital owned by a religious entity who only allowed us to wear one of five colors and no patterns to work. At the end of two years, when it was time for me to move on, I looked in the mirror and truly did not recognize myself.) So where is the line between too much authenticity and just right for the workplace? Stacy London in her book, *The Truth About Style*, says

> I like a 75-25 split: 75 percent of your style choices should be about making you happy; 25 percent can be about what you're transmitting to others and making a good impression to help you get what you want out of life.[14]

I think this advice is spot-on, not only for professional dress style choices, but also for how much authenticity is appropriate in the workplace. How you portray yourself on social media, in person, in email, and over the phone should be win-win for both you and your fans. It should engender and foster trust. It should move you closer to achieving your professional goals; all the while helping your fans solve their problems with products and services that add value.

When I was a little girl, my mom taught train-the-trainer classes at our church and I was her assistant. I helped put up the bulletin boards and organize the transparency films. To this day I still remember that she always closed her classes with a call for authenticity. She encouraged the other teachers to be real with their students and she would read a passage from *The Velveteen Rabbit*. I share that passage with you now in the hopes it will inspire you as much as it did me to take the risk to be real.

'Real isn't how you are made', said the Skin Horse. 'It's a thing that happens to you. When a child loves you for a long, long time, not just to play with, but REALLY loves you, then you become Real.'

'Does it hurt?' asked the Rabbit.

'Sometimes', said the Skin Horse, for he was always truthful. When you are Real you don't mind being hurt.

'Does it happen all at once, like being wound up', he asked, or 'bit by bit'?

'It doesn't happen all at once', said the Skin Horse. 'You become. It takes a long time. That's why it doesn't happen often to people who break easily, or have sharp edges, or who have to be *carefully kept. Generally, by the time you are Real, most of your hair has been loved off, and your eyes drop out and you get loose in the joints and very shabby. But these things don't matter at all, because once you are Real you can't be ugly, except to people who don't understand."[15]*

FORMULATE YOUR GAME PLAN

Five FANtastic Questions to Help You Become More Authentic

----

1. What is more of a challenge for you: 1) Letting people in to get
    to know the real you or 2) Maintaining professional boundaries
    to ensure an appropriate level of authenticity for the workplace?

    _____

    _____

    _____

    _____

    _____

    _____

2. Of the four trust breakers mentioned, which one do you struggle
    with the most? What is one action step you could take to improve
    that behavior?

    _____

    _____

    _____

    _____

    _____

    _____

    _____

3. In addition to the four trust breakers mentioned, what other trust breakers have you observed salespeople committing? What impact did that have on the relationship with their fans?

_____

_____

_____

_____

_____

_____

_____

_____

4. List three of your most trusted brands. What did they do or say to earn and keep your trust?

_____

_____

_____

_____

_____

_____

_____

_____

5. Imagine you found yourself in a situation similar to what I described at the very beginning of this chapter. What sales-related skills and experiences could you draw upon to de-escalate and resolve the situation?

nur·tur·ing
to support and encourage

How FANtastic is your follow-up?

HOW MANY OF YOU HAVE been shopping for a bra recently? My girlfriend told me if I wanted the best bra to go to Nordstrom and ask for the iBra as seen on Oprah. So there I am standing in the lingerie department at Nordstrom when I make eye-contact with Wendy the salesperson who appeared to be warming her hands and cracking her knuckles at the sight of me. Little did I know that selling bras is an intimate, personal, and hands-on experience! Here's the rest of the story...

As she escorted me to the dressing room, she informed me she was a Certified Bra Fitting Specialist. (Yes, that's a real job!) She measured, she lifted, she separated, she all but gave me a mammogram and, before I knew it, I was wearing the best-fitting bra of all time. I wanted to ask her why it was called an iBra; did it have apps and require charging? Then I figured it out—it must be wireless! (I know bad, bad joke.) At this point I feel like Wendy and I are best friends so there is nothing left to do but buy the bra. Wendy rings up the sale and asks me to fill out a registration card so she can stay in touch. Since there had already been so much touching, I figured a little more couldn't hurt, and I filled out the form.

A week goes by; I open up my mailbox to retrieve the mail and there is a handwritten note from Wendy with her business card. Wow! How nice of her to remember me! A few more weeks go by, I open up the mailbox, sort through the junk mail and find another handwritten note from Wendy. More weeks go by, and Wendy continues to stay in touch. Triple wow! Either Wendy is the greatest salesperson of all time or I am being stalked by the bra lady at Nordstrom!

The sixth trait of a rock-star, top-producing, quota-busting FANtastic salesperson is the ability to be nurturing. Nurturing relationships means you care enough to follow up and follow through. We discussed follow-through in Chapter Five so in this chapter we will focus on follow-up. FANtastic follow-up is a lost art. Out of all of the ideas discussed in the book, FANtastic follow-up is perhaps the easiest one to adopt and the one with the greatest potential to set you apart in the market place.

THE FOLLOW-UP DISCONNECT

The fact is 44% of salespeople give up after one follow-up attempt[16] and yet 80% of sales require five to six follow-up attempts after the meeting.[17] See the disconnect? Even more concerning, FollowUpSuccess.com found in a study[18] that:

- 48% of salespeople never follow up with a prospect
- 25% of salespeople make a second contact and stop
- 12% of salespeople make more than three contacts

Sirius Decisions claims that the average salesperson only makes two attempts to reach a prospect.[19] I doubt you would argue with me that nurturing relationships with creative, memorable, personalized follow-up is critical to converting more prospects to purchasers. So why the disconnect? Why do we fail to follow up? When I ask salespeople at my workshops and seminars, I get a range of answers.

- Fear of rejection
- Fear of being perceived as too pushy
- Too busy with other tasks
- Laziness
- Lack of organization

All, some, or none of these reasons may be true, but I suspect for most salespeople the core issue is you don't get results from your follow-up so it seems like a waste of time. I do not believe most salespeople are lazy, disorganized, thin-skinned procrastinators who just don't do their follow-up because they don't care. Particularly salespeople like yourself who would take the time and energy to read a book on how to improve their sales skills. Furthermore, the sales educators who advocate those theories are frankly insulting. In my experience, the reason you fail to consistently follow up is because the response rate to your emails, voice mails, and handwritten notes is so low that it doesn't seem like it is a good use of your time. So you forgo follow-up in lieu of other tasks that deliver an immediate, more satisfying return. How did I do? Sound familiar?

Be honest with yourself. On a scale of 1 to 10, how consistent and persistent are you with follow-up? If you scored yourself less than a 9 or 10, what is the reason for your lack of follow-up? Psychologist and television host Dr. Phil McGraw often says, "You can't change what you don't acknowledge." He is so right. Take a moment for some inner reflection and be brutally honest with yourself as to why you fail to follow up.

FANTASTIC FOLLOW-UP STRATEGY #1—RESPOND QUICKLY

Now that we have established the need for follow-up and explored the reasons why we fail to execute it, this next section is going to give you five strategies to help you improve your follow-up. Each strategy has the same goal in mind: to increase the prospect's response rate to your follow-up efforts. I believe that if more prospects start returning your follow-up calls and responding to your emails that you will be motivated, incentivized, and frankly excited to make follow-up a daily priority.

The first rule of FANtastic follow-up is to respond quickly. Timing is everything especially if you are responsible for following up with website generated leads. **You can't be too fast. You can only be too slow.** Research at InsideSales.com found that if you follow up with web leads within five minutes, you are nine times more likely to convert them, and that 50% of sales go to the first salesperson to contact the prospect.[20] Unfortunately, the response to website leads by most companies is abysmal. The 2015 Eptica Multichannel Customer Experience Study found that UK businesses are failing to answer up to 50% of customer-service inquiries delivered via online channels.[21] Forbes paints an even bleaker picture in a study they conducted over five years, secretly shopping 10,000 company websites. On average, companies took 46 hours and 53 minutes to pick up the phone and respond to a lead. The conclusion of the study was that 71% of websites are wasted due to a slow response time or no response at all[22]. Wow.

The reason web leads, who I believe on some level are already FANS of your product, service or brand, do not respond to your emails and phone calls is because you are responding too slowly. It is not because they are tire kickers who are not really interested. Andy Paul, author of the award-winning book, *Zero-Time Selling: 10 Essential Steps to Accelerate Every Company's Sales*, nailed it with this quote, "...[the] majority of salespeople still view in-bound sales leads with hesitant suspicion instead of welcoming them as a source of substantially pre-educated sales interest that they typically are in this Internet age." If you still believe web leads are a waste of time, please go back to Chapter One and re-read it until you believe me!

How fast do you need to be? An ideal response time for a website lead is within minutes of the request. InsideSales.com concludes that the odds of reaching a lead by phone decrease by over 10 times in the first hour. The odds of qualifying a lead decrease by over six times in the first hour. The odds of contacting a lead if called in five minutes versus 30 minutes drops 100 times. The odds of qualifying a lead if called in five minutes versus 30 minutes drops 21 times.[23] In a 2011 article titled, *The Short Life of Online Sales Leads*, Harvard Business Review reports

> *...U.S. Firms that tried to contact potential customers within an hour of receiving a query were nearly seven times as likely to qualify the lead (which we defined as having a meaningful conversation with a key decision maker) as those that tried to contact the customer even an hour later—and more than 60 times as likely as companies that waited 24 hours or longer.[24]*

The need for speed places an unfair burden on salespeople who are otherwise engaged throughout the day with client appointments, sales meetings, and networking events. In Chapter Four we talked about the importance of giving your fans your complete undivided attention so you could pick up on personalization clues to make the sales experience engaging. How are you supposed to respond within seconds to a website inquiry when you are busy talking to other fans all day? The best answer to this conundrum is for your company to utilize an Online Sales Counselor (OSC) to respond, manage, and nurture all website leads. An Online Sales Counselor is an inside sales position solely dedicated to responding, nurturing, and managing web leads. I talk about how to implement an Online Sales Counselor program at length in two of my other books, *Click Power: The Proven System Home Builders Use to Drive More Traffic, Leads, and Sales*, and *FANtastic Marketing: Leverage Your Fan Factor, Build a Blockbuster Brand, Score New Customers, and Wipe Out the Competition*. Since so many of my readers are loyal and have already read those books, I won't duplicate the information here for fear of repeating myself. If you haven't read those books, and you are interested in the program, simply drop me an email and I'll send you that information. Bottom line—if you have at least 50 website leads per month, you can justify and see a return on investment by implementing an OSC. If you are a small business, solopreneur, or not quite up to 50 website leads a month, then you need to develop a process to respond faster. Find someone in your office perhaps who is sitting at a computer for most of the day and can respond immediately. Develop a queue system that designates one person per day as the website rapid response person. Find a way to respond faster and you will convert more website leads into sales.

FANTASTIC FOLLOW-UP STRATEGY #2—FOLLOW UP MORE THAN ONCE

How much follow-up is enough? Until they buy, die, or get a restraining order, of course! I'm kidding, but the fact is 80% of sales require five follow-up calls after the meeting and sadly 44% of salespeople give up after one follow-up.[25] Followupsuccess.com concludes:

- 2% of sales are made on the first contact.
- 3% of sales are made on the second contact.
- 5% of sales are made on the third contact.

- 10% of sales are made on the fourth contact.
- 80% of sales are made on the fifth to twelfth contact.[26]

I recommend your follow-up process include six follow-up attempts. Let's say for example, your typical buying cycle is 45 days long. The follow-up schedule would look like this:

- Follow-up #1—Same day as initial contact via email or hand-written note
- Follow-up #2—Day 3 after initial contact via phone
- Follow-up #3—Day 7 after initial contact via email
- Follow-up #4—Day 14 after initial contact via phone
- Follow-up #5—Day 30 after initial contact via phone
- Follow-up #6—Day 45 after initial contact via email
- Ongoing—Once a month email to entire database

I can't recommend a specific follow-up schedule that will be perfect for every reader because it must be completely customized to your fan base. I can give you several principles to use when determining your follow-up process. First, the follow-up attempts should be spaced out over the typical buying cycle of your product or service. If you have a long buying cycle, then you may need more than six follow-up attempts and you will need to spread them out further. Be careful spacing them out too much because you don't want the fans to forget who you are and delete your messages as spam. Second, never ever follow-up more than once a day. Third, use the fan's preferred communication channel (email, phone, text), but if after a few follow-up attempts you are not getting a response, try a different communication channel and reach out at a different time of day. We'll talk more about this in Strategy #5 below. Fourth, please note the six follow-up attempts are one-to-one follow-up attempts. Dumping the name into your group email blast does not count as follow-up and it won't work. However, if you still do not receive a response after completing six one-to-one follow-up attempts, don't abandon the lead completely. Add the name to your email marketing database and send at least one group email a month that includes product updates, company news, and industry information.

How many follow-up attempts are you currently doing? I'm willing to bet it isn't six. Why not? Probably because you are trying to use a manual system like Post-It Notes®, spreadsheets, or handwritten reminders on a paper calendar. Unfortunately, once you build up a volume of leads to follow up with, manual systems will fail because they are too cumbersome and time consuming to be worth the effort. **In order to be truly effective with lead follow-up, you must learn to appreciate and utilize automated processes within your CRM (Customer Relationship Management) software.** I know most salespeople hate using CRM software. You feel like big brother (AKA management) is monitoring you and using the data in the CRM software against you to determine if you are hitting performance benchmarks. So you sandbag the data and only feed information into the software that will make you look good on the weekly sales report. If that doesn't sound familiar, perhaps you feel that using the CRM takes longer and slows you down compared to your own system. Lastly, some salespeople tell me they simply aren't comfortable with the CRM technology and haven't received any or enough training to be proficient using it. Whatever the reason, I know that salespeople and CRM are like oil and water. Most just don't like using it. I get it. But like a lot of things that are good for us—eating broccoli, working out, getting enough sleep—sometimes we have to just do it even when we don't like it.

What if I could reframe your perception of CRM software? What if I could help you think about it differently? What if I could help you see the benefit of using it? Let's start with the very definition. What does CRM stand for? Say it with me...**C**ustomer **R**elationship **M**anagement. Yes, this is the traditional and correct definition. But what if CRM stood for something else? What if it stood for...wait for it—**C**ash **R**ecovery **M**achine! Your CRM software is like an ATM for your sales. Your future pipeline of sales is in the software. Your job is to mine the database on a daily basis to extract the cash. Instead of loathing your CRM, I want you to start visualizing cash flying out of your computer screen and straight into your pocket or purse! I literally want you to start seeing dollar signs every time you use it. Because the truth is, if you use it routinely, you will start to convert more of your fans into buyers. Once they become buyers you can convert them into raving fans who will bring you more buyers. See how that works?

In order for your CRM to be a cash recovery machine, every single lead, all prospects, all ups, all guests, and all fans must be entered into the system. No more sandbagging (a term that means you only enter selected leads into the system to make your numbers look better). This also means sales management must stop grading your performance solely on conversion statistics.

I understand that when you are solely judged on lead-to-sales conversions it is incredibly tempting to only enter the A+ prospects into the system. But you have to resist temptation and enter every single lead. Why? Because the follow-up system I am advocating works on percentages. The bigger the number of leads coming into the top end of the funnel, the higher number you will convert. Also, your marketing department desperately needs accurate traffic counts if they are to make smart decisions regarding marketing. They need to know how many total leads were generated and what traffic source prompted their interest. If you want the marketing department to generate qualified traffic and genuine interest for your product or service, then you must do your part and enter every single lead into the CRM. Period.

I am frequently asked what is the best CRM? Great question. The best CRM is...*the one you use!* I wish there was a perfect CRM on the market, one that has zero flaws, is lightning fast, and is super easy to use. But no such perfect product exists. I've worked with countless CRM programs and while it is definitely true some are better than others, I have yet to find a perfect option. It is easy to blame your current system for your lack of use but I promise that if your company invested thousands of dollars and hundreds of hours converting to a new CRM program, within a short period of time you would find flaws with that one as well. As Crosby, Stills, and Nash sang so beautifully in the '70s, when it comes to CRM, learn to "love the one you're with." The grass is not greener on another computer.

FANTASTIC FOLLOW-UP STRATEGY #3—STOP CHECKING IN

I mentioned earlier in this chapter that I believe the number one reason why salespeople do not consistently follow up with leads is because they do not get a response from most of them. We addressed one reason for a lack of response in Strategy #1—you are responding too slowly. The other major reason you don't receive a response is because your follow-up is all about you and not them. Stop reading for a moment and pull up your most recent five follow-up emails. Re-read them. How many times per follow-up attempt did you talk about yourself, your product, or your brand? Now compare that to the number of times you referenced the fan's interests, needs, and desires? Do you see the disconnect? Reverse positions and if you were the lead, would you respond?

I established in Chapter Four that we respond to messages that are personalized and customized to us. This applies not only to the initial sales conversation but also to follow-up messages. Yet, most salespeople send emails and handwritten notes that say things like "It was a pleasure to meet you" or "I enjoyed learning about your company today." While pleasant sounding, who are those messages really about? They are about you! And frankly, your fans don't really care if you enjoyed meeting them or if it was a pleasure to learn more about them because it's your job to care. You are supposed to care. **Your follow-up response rate will dramatically increase when you make the follow-up about the fan and not about you.** In order to make the follow-up about the fan, you will need detailed notes from the conversation (back to Chapter 4 again) and you will need to keep those notes in a centralized place where you can easily access them. That's right, we are back to why you need to use CRM!

Avoid using cliché phrases like "checking in" and "touching base" in your follow-up messages. Why? Because they sound like a sales pitch and scream "this is a form letter." When you receive an email or voicemail from a salesperson who says "I'm just checking in" or "Just wanted to touch base", what do you do? Delete! So what are you supposed to say? I recommend using some variation of this phrase:

- I was thinking about our meeting last week and called to tell you...
- You mentioned _____ in a conversation yesterday and I wanted to share with you...
- I was thinking about your need to _____ and thought this might be of value to you...

Do you hear the common theme in those statements? The common theme is "I was thinking about you" (in a non-creepy way of course!). When your follow-up demonstrates that you care, that you are thinking about your fans and their needs, you will receive a response. I guarantee it. Maybe not after one attempt—it may take all six attempts—but at some point, generally around the fourth or fifth attempt, you will get a response.

When you connect the dots of a previous conversation and add something new of value to the conversation, your chances of receiving a response skyrocket. **Bottom line, stop checking in**

and touching base, and start adding value. How do you add value to a follow-up message?

1. **Share an Idea or Insight**—Based on your first conversation with the fan, share a new idea or insight in your follow-up message. For example, "We talked about your need to cut printing costs during our meeting, so I thought I would share this article on our blog about budget-friendly brochure and business card options." With this approach, you are building upon the first conversation with new value-added information that the fan may not have access to or have considered. If your website has interactive tools, such as how-to videos, price calculators, checklists, white-paper case studies and/or educational blog articles, use them to educate your fans and, in the process, drive traffic back to your website.

2. **Solve a Problem**—Another option to add value to your follow-up is to offer a solution to a challenge mentioned in the first conversation. FANtastic salespeople are always listening to their fans concerns, challenges, and objections. Document those concerns in your CRM notes and when it is time for a follow-up you can reference that challenge and offer a solution, resource, or idea to help solve it. Take, for example, a moving company selling moving services direct to consumers. A follow-up message that seeks to solve a problem would sound like this: "You mentioned a concern about your mother being able to unpack once she arrived at her new home. I thought you might be interested to know we

offer unpacking services and if she prefers to do it herself, here is a link to an article with useful unpacking tips."

3. **Ask a Question**—If you want to receive a response to your follow-up call, text or email, you have to engage in a dialogue not a monologue. A dialogue requires that you ask a question of the other person to illicit a response. As we discussed in Chapter Three, your question has to be thoughtful, genuinely inquisitive, and not a clichéd, overly *salesy* question. You will not get a response to over-used, trite questions, because they seem disingenuous at best and lazy at worst. Reference the first conversation you had with the fan and ask a follow-up question based on that information. The question could be an alternative-choice type question that asks them to pick one option over another. Using the moving company example again, "Are you looking for a portable storage solution or fixed storage for your corporate relocations?" Another option is to ask for feedback on the conversation so far, "Based on our discussion on Tuesday, what is your feedback on our solution meeting your needs?" Lastly, you can also ask a next-steps or timeframe question, such as "Now that we've gone over our solutions, what do you see as your next step?"

FANTASTIC FOLLOW-UP STRATEGY #4—TONE MATTERS

I recently received the following email from someone I have never met, talked to, or frankly heard of.

RE: my last attempt

Hi Meredith,

I have tried contacting you 3 times now since we connected on LinkedIn. I know you are busy, but I do think it will be well worth your time for us to explore opportunities that we can both benefit from. I can't tell you how often I have not followed-up and then wondered "Did I let another opportunity fall through the cracks?" So I thought I would try one more time to set up a quick discovery call with you. If I don't hear back from you about setting up a meeting, you won't hear from me again. So if you have the time, hit reply and let me know some times that work best for you. I will work around your schedule.

John Smith
ABC Company

How did the tone of that email strike you? I might be overly sensitive, but the first sentence came across as scolding to me. Then the next sentence presumed to know what was best for me, as if I don't know that for myself. The last half of the email isn't that bad, but most people wouldn't make it that far because I think they would be so turned off by the opening.

Apparently this individual scraped my email address from my LinkedIn profile and dumped it into his email marketing program. Don't do that! That is not okay. Just because you are connected on LinkedIn does not give you permission to add the person to your email database. To make matters worse, he began spamming me with these cold-call email letters. By the time I received the one above, I was annoyed enough to save it to my files as an example of a serious sales **don't** for my speeches and books. This email is not about me, the fan. This email is not FANtastic selling. This email is obnoxious selling at its finest.

You might be thinking, how is this email any different than the six follow-up attempts you are recommending? It is very different. First, I am recommending you follow-up six times ONLY with people who have expressed an interest first. Second, all of your follow-up must be individualized and personalized. You can draft some follow-up letter templates in your CRM to save time and use them as a starting point for your follow-up, but you should also take the time to add value to each follow-up by sharing an idea or insight, solving a problem, and/or asking a question.

The tone you use when you follow up is so important. Even though you have followed up many times before, you should never sound annoyed or put out that you are following up again. Erase those previous attempts from your mind and reach out with the same level of enthusiasm and professionalism as attempt number one. A sales training colleague and close personal friend of mine, Kerry Mulcrone of Kerry and Co., often asks her audiences when it comes to email and voicemail, "Can they hear your smile?" Remember that email is tone deaf, resulting in many ways to interpret the tone of the words in the email. You have to amp up the energy and enthusiasm to make sure the recipient can hear your smile on the other end of the send button. This does not mean using a lot of smiley emoticons and purple curlicue fonts in your email. The email format and wording should be professional, but the overall tone should be friendly and warm.

FANTASTIC FOLLOW-UP STRATEGY #5—CHANGE THE CHANNEL

My final tip to help you increase your follow-up response rate is to be more strategic about the communication channel you use for follow-up. By communication channel, I mean email, voicemail, text, instant message, handwritten note, etc. **Most salespeople use the communication channel they personally prefer instead of using the channel that the fan prefers.** We each have a communication channel preference. Some of us are phone people—we prefer a quick phone call over an email or text. Others never, ever pick up the phone and prefer to text. Some never respond to their work email, but respond lightening fast to a Facebook Messenger chat. FANtastic salespeople set their own communication channel preferences and biases aside and select the channel preferred by the fan. Just because the phone, for example, works best for you, doesn't mean it works best for the fan you are trying to reach.

Several years ago, when I was in need of new headshots, I reached out through Facebook Messenger to a photographer whom I had met several times at various networking events. I stated specifically that I wanted to hire him and offered several dates/times I was available and asked for his availability. Instead of responding back via Facebook Messenger with several availability options, his response was for me to call his office so we could talk further. The problem with that response was that I was going to be gone for several days in a different time zone and my time to make or take phone calls was going to be limited. I knew I was going to be hard to reach by phone if I didn't reach him on the first attempt. His response put the work back on me and in most cases, when you ask the fan to do the work, it will result in the fan walking away from the sale. In your first conversation with every fan you must establish what is his or her communication channel preference. Then it is incumbent on you to be flexible enough to communicate in a way that they prefer.

If, after several attempts using their preferred communication channel, you still haven't reached them, then consider changing the channel. Change up the time of day and day of the week. Use a little humor and have some fun. As long as you don't sound annoyed or scolding, don't be afraid to let your personality, energy, and enthusiasm shine through.

APPLY NOW

Whew! That's a lot of information for one chapter. I'm exhausted writing it all much less trying to put it into action. Here's the thing about follow-up: it really only works when you do it. I would rather you do consistent follow-up that is timely and persistent versus perfect follow-up where every message is crafted carefully to read like an expensive greeting card. In fact, most salespeople tell me the shorter the message, the higher the response rate. So you don't have to write *War and Peace*-length emails or leave ten-minute voice mails. But what you must do is make it about them. Drop the clichés. Follow-up immediately. Follow-up more than once. If you do those things and they can hear your smile between the lines of the message, you will get a response. And a response will turn into a sale.

FORMULATE YOUR GAME PLAN

Five FANtastic Questions to Help You Become More Nurturing

----

1. Do you need to focus more on responding more quickly to leads, customizing your message to the fans, or adding more follow-up attempts to your process?

2. Do you have a CRM system? If yes, how do you really feel about it? Can you consider the possibility it could be a Cash Recovery Machine for you if used properly or fully? What is one action step that needs to happen for you to be able to use it more fully?

 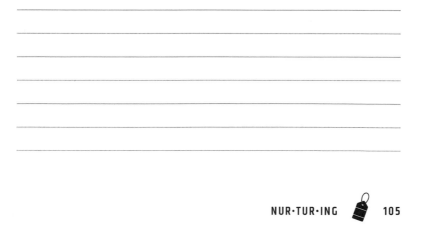

3. If you answered no to Question #2, what is one action step you need to take to implement a CRM system, either for yourself personally or for your company?

_____

_____

_____

_____

_____

_____

_____

_____

4. What is your current follow-up process? How many times do you typically continue to follow up after an initial conversation? Is that current process working for you? What is your current follow-up response rate?

_____

_____

_____

_____

_____

_____

_____

_____

5. What communication channel do you prefer? How rigid or how flexible are you in regard to using other channels? Is there a channel you need to learn more about or become more familiar with so you can use it when needed?

_____

_____

_____

_____

_____

_____

_____

_____

so·cia·ble

willing to talk and engage in activities with other people;
friendly

How well do you leverage your
Fan Factor to build relationships
and make sales?

I WILL NEVER FORGET MY first concert. I was fourteen years old, living in Orlando, Florida, and I begged my parents to see Bon Jovi. It was the height of the 1980s and I don't know whose hair was bigger, mine or Jon Bon Jovi's. I was a preacher's kid at the time and my parents reluctantly allowed me to go to the concert on two conditions: 1) I couldn't tell anyone from church we were going, for fear of recrimination; and 2) We would sneak in after the opening act started, when it was already dark, so we wouldn't draw attention to ourselves. The plan was going great until the local news crew covering the opening night of the new venue spotted my parents in the atrium and interviewed them LIVE for the local evening news! Here's the rest of the story...

Once my brother and I were settled in our seats, my parents excused themselves to get a cup of coffee and walk around the atrium until the concert was over. That's when the local news reporter spotted them and rushed over with lights and a camera crew and asked for their reaction to the grand opening of the brand new Orlando O-rena (instead of "arena" the venue was nicknamed "O-rena"). Needless to say, the last thing my father wanted was to be on the news that evening for fear someone in the congregation would see we had attended the rock concert. Never at a loss for words, my father stepped up to the mic and simply said, "Aren't we all just living on a prayer?" Bam, drop the mic!

Since that experience I've been an unabashed Bon Jovi fan. If Bon Jovi performs within 200 miles of my zip code, I go to the concert. I play their music when I am cleaning, working out, and writing (they are playing right now!). I've been a fan of many things during my life, but none have outlasted my love for Bon Jovi. Whenever I play their music, I am reminded of that night's antics, how awesome my parents are, and what it feels like to be a teenager with a crush on a rock star.

The idea for **The Fan Factor**™ came to me at a 2005 Bon Jovi concert in Raleigh, North Carolina. Between songs, the band thanked the audience for helping them attain 12 million fans on Facebook (the page is currently at 26 million fans) and offered their Facebook fans an exclusive behind-the-scenes video available only on Facebook after the concert. Upon hearing this, I took out my iPhone, opened my Notes app and typed "The Fan Factor." By acknowledging, thanking, and rewarding their loyal fans with a special video, Bon Jovi further cemented the already adoring relationship between them and the 17,000 screaming fans in the arena that night.

In that moment, I understood how to effectively marry social media and business. When you make it about the fans, when you give the fans what they want online, they pay attention. You see, no matter how busy I am, what time of day it is, or how many deadlines I have, if I see a Facebook post by or about Bon Jovi, I stop and read it. Why? Because I'm a fan. And fans make time for the objects of their affection no matter how busy or distracted they might be. But it doesn't stop with simply getting your fan's attention. When you go the extra mile to acknowledge, thank, and reward your fans, they become an extension of your sales team. **Once your fans become engaged, loyal, and utterly rabid about you, they start doing the selling and marketing for you.** That is the essence of The Fan Factor principle.

The Fan Factor is at work when your fans start posting rave reviews about working with you throughout the sales process. The Fan Factor is at work when your fans refer other fans via word-of-mouth and *word-of-mouse* on social media. The Fan Factor is at work when your fans repeat your personal brand message back to you as a verb. You know you are a FANtastic salesperson when you connect so strongly with your fans that the fans do the selling and marketing for you.

You may not be a Bon Jovi fan (I can't imagine why not), but, I'm willing to bet there is something or someone you drop everything to hear, read or learn more about. From cooking to comic books, music to movies, dogs to decorating, sports to soap operas, everyone is a fan of something. If you tap into your own fan behaviors you can learn a lot about The Fan Factor.

Social media, when used correctly, is a FANtastic tool for building your own personal Fan Factor. Before social media you had limited options for building relationships with your fans—primarily phone calls and in-person meetings. While both of those tools are incredibly valuable, sometimes it is impossible to reach your fans by phone or nail down a few minutes for an in-person meeting. With social media, you can simply *like* one of your fan's LinkedIn posts about a promotion or write a quick note of congratulations on Facebook for a milestone event like a birthday or anniversary. Every social media interaction, no matter how small, further solidifies your relationship and adds a new dimension to it. When you have a solid relationship with your fans, the result is that they actually pay attention to your messages, even your sales messages, which are typically ignored. If you want your fans to stop deleting your emails and voicemails, learn how to make The Fan Factor work for you.

The seventh undeniable trait of a rock-star, top-producing, quota-busting FANtastic salesperson is the ability to be sociable. Of course being sociable at in-person meetings and networking events is incredibly important, but for the purposes of this chapter I am going to focus on being sociable on social media. The ultimate result is that the Fan Factor goes to work for you, ensuring your fans pay attention, focus, refer, and buy from you. And remember, I define fans as not only your current loyal customers, but also your interested prospects who have agreed to interact with you even though they haven't purchased yet. (Go back to Chapter One if you need a refresher on that concept—it's an important one.)

Most of the authors, sales trainers, and sales leadership experts use the term *social selling* to refer to the concept of using social media as a sales tool. The highest and best use of social selling is to nurture, enhance, and develop relationships with your fans. In other words, be sociable. Social media allows you to position yourself as the go-to expert, a trusted advisor, who knows how to solve a clearly defined set of problems.

Using social media as the modern-day cold call completely misses the point of social media. At least once a week I get a cold-call message via LinkedIn, Facebook, or Instagram pitching me a product or service from a person I don't know. How many of those do you think I've responded to? Exactly ZERO.

You might be thinking—wait a minute, I am connected to a lot of people on social media that I have never met and/or don't know well, so why not blast and bury those connections with sales messages? The reason is because you are connected through something or someone you have in common. At least you should be connected for a reason; your social media connections and followers should be in line with your fan base. Targeted connections can be developed into meaningful relationships. However, if you oversell instead of being sociable, the relationship will fizzle fast.

Don't get me wrong, I believe in networking and prospecting. Sales rock stars have a large sphere of influence and are constantly adding new people to it. If you need to build a bigger sphere of influence, get out from behind your desk and go do some in-person networking, i.e., join an association, join a leads group, or join a community service group. To put it simply, get out and meet people! Once you meet someone, if you find a mutual interest, connect on social media. Build that relationship over time with consistent interaction and at some point it will make sense to do business together. You will not substantially increase your sales by essentially cold calling on social media, because the point of social media is to connect with the people we already know and get to know them better. It's to be sociable!

DO I HAVE TO?

For those of you not using social media to be sociable with your fans, you are missing out on the most popular and heavily utilized communication channel since Al Gore invented the internet (just kidding!). Consider these facts from the LinkedIn 2016 State of Sales Survey:

- More than 70% of sales professionals use social selling tools, including LinkedIn, Twitter and Facebook, making them the most widely used sales technology. Specifically, sales professionals see relationship-building tools as having the highest impact on revenue.
- 90% of top salespeople use social selling tools, compared with 71% of overall sales professionals.

- Millennials are 33% more likely to use sales-intelligence tools, which generate background and contact information on leads, than industry peers aged 35-54.

I frequently hear objections such as, "I don't have time for social networking" or "I don't know how." The truth is a lack of time and skill are no longer acceptable excuses. Remember, old ways of marketing and selling no longer work. If they aren't working, you can't use them to make sales. You have little choice but to learn how to use social networking to build relationships with your fans. Who knows, in time you might enjoy it.

I confess I was one of the skeptics. I vividly remember a conversation with a fellow colleague where I told her that salespeople would never use social networking and it should be relegated to the marketing department at the corporate level. She was very patient with me and has never come back to say "I told you so!" even though she has every right to do so.

If you are feeling overwhelmed by the thought of interacting on social media, that's okay. I've felt that way too. All sales and marketing professionals have. There are so many tasks, and not enough hands to do them, and deadlines looming all around us. But, in our heart of hearts, that is why we are in the field. We thrive on and enjoy the adrenalin rush of a lot of things happening at once. If this seems like too much with your current responsibilities, slow down for a moment. Take a deep breath and focus on the following sociable strategies, one at a time. Keep your action steps simple and attainable. Set a goal to improve and then pick the book back up to work on the next strategy.

STRATEGY #1—POST WITH PURPOSE

Here's the good news. You do not need to participate on every available social media channel. If you enjoy social media, want to participate on a lot of channels, and have a high degree of technical skills, more power to you! Go for it! My business has certainly benefited from a large social media footprint. For those of you feeling overwhelmed, I would encourage you to select two to three social media channels that match your fan base and that suit your technical abilities and participate in those channels consistently.

Where do your fans typically "hang out" online? If you aren't sure, ask them! Make social media part of your sales process. Ask your fans what social media channels they use and ask permission to connect during your very first sales conversation.

In addition to asking your fans what channels they use, you can also draw conclusions from surveys on social media usage. The Pew Research Center recently completed a national survey of 1,520 adults and found the following user statistics[27].

- 79% of internet users (68% of all U.S. adults) use Facebook.
- 32% of internet users (28% of all U.S. adults) use Instagram.
- 24% of internet users (21% of all U.S. adults) use Twitter.
- 29% of internet users (25% of all U.S. adults) use LinkedIn.
- 31% of internet users (26% of all U.S. adults) use Pinterest.

The study also looked at the demographic profiles for each channel. Facebook is more heavily used by women ranging from 18—65+. Instagram and Twitter are more popular with younger adults ages 18—29. LinkedIn tends to be popular with college graduates and high-income earners. Last but not least, Pinterest is a powerhouse for the female audience, using the site at double the share of online men.

The point of sharing these statistics is to help you understand that each social media channel has its own audience and should be used accordingly. Social media websites are like channels on your television. Is the programming on ESPN and HGTV the same? No, of course not! Most successful television channels have a well-defined audience and the programming delivered is meant to appeal to that audience. Ask your fans which channels they use and marry that with the research above. Now, which two to three channels should you focus on to build your Fan Factor?

The last consideration in the selection of your social media channels is your own technical expertise and communication style. Have you read the book *Now, Discover Your Strengths* by Marcus Buckingham? It's several years old, but still powerful and relevant. In the book, Buckingham makes the point that we often focus on improving our weaknesses rather than further enhancing and leveraging our strengths. His research found that career success comes from our strengths not our attempts to mitigate our weaknesses. I couldn't agree more. If you love to use your camera to take photos and film videos, then Instagram and YouTube are perfect channels for you. But if you would rather die than be in a selfie video then don't do it! If tweeting multiple times a day and the snarky tone of Twitter makes your blood boil, don't do it. Select another channel. If you love to write, then start a blog. However, if you can't put three coherent sentences together and struggle with writing basic emails, why are you trying to blog and shaming yourself in the process? Stop the madness! If cat videos and vacation photos drive you crazy, then Facebook is not for you. It's okay. Review the culture and communication style of each social media channel and match that to your own communication style and technical abilities. This ensures that you will consistently be present on the channels and not procrastinate because you dread participating. My prediction is that once your start seeing results from being sociable on social media, you will be willing to push yourself to learn additional channels. There is nothing like success as a motivation factor.

STRATEGY #2—MAKE IT ABOUT THE FANS

If you are already using social media to build relationships with your fans then your next opportunity is to refine what you are already doing. One common mistake I see with salespeople is overselling on social media. I touched on this at the beginning of this chapter with my lecture about cold calling on social media. Overselling goes beyond cold calling. The Convince and Convert blog said it perfectly in a blog post titled *The Key to Social Selling is Social, Not Selling*. "It's called social selling because it's about connecting socially first (as you would during a trade show, dinner meeting, or at the bar) and selling second."[28]

What is your current ratio of sales messages versus non-sales messages on social media? Have you ever connected with a sales person on social media only to see post after post promoting a new product or service? How long did you stay connected? Probably not long. My husband remarked recently, "The problem with social media is that companies and salespeople only use it to try and sell you something. When you have a legitimate problem and need help, they are strikingly unresponsive." Well said.

Your current customers are already sold. That's why they chose to buy from you and connect with you on social media. And remember, even the prospects who haven't purchased yet are on some level a fan. Maybe they haven't purchased yet, but they are at least sold on learning more about you. How long they remain a fan is directly determined by what you do next.

Think of it this way. DVR owners use the device to watch television on their own timetable and, most importantly, to skip the commercials. If all you do is post sales content on social media then you are making it about you and not the fans. At that point you are nothing more than a commercial and your fans will tune you out.

I believe in an 80/20 rule for social selling content. 80% of your content should be non-sales messages and 20% should be sales messages. I define a non-sales message as content that doesn't directly pitch, promote, or ask someone to buy your product or service. Does that mean 80% of your posts are cat videos, political memes, and pictures of your dinner? Absolutely not. Within the 80% of non-sales messages you can absolutely soft-sell yourself and your products with what I call "work light" types of posts. Live the experience of your work online and share your daily experiences. Show your fans how much you love your work, your company, and your customers.

For some of you, 100% of your posts are non-sales messages because you are afraid to be perceived as pushy. This is as big a mistake as overselling. If you have a solid relationship with your fans, they want to know how to buy from you. They want to know when you have new products and services available. They want to be the first to buy from you and actively refer you. Like most things, the magic is the balance between the sales and non-sales messages. Overdoing it or not doing enough will defeat the purpose of being sociable on social media for business.

Fans want to find solutions to their problems and escape the challenges of everyday life. Your non-sales content should also add value and be meaningful to your fans. Does your content offer authentic answers about problems and challenges your fans are dealing with?

The first step to developing a sociable social-selling strategy is determining what value you will provide your fans. What valuable insights will your fans care about?

Many sales people I consult with are concerned that they don't have anything of value to say. This is a natural and common feeling. You probably don't think of yourself as an expert in your field, but the truth is, after you've worked in a particular position or industry for a reasonable length of time, you develop a specialized skill set that others will find valuable. Tap into your knowledge base and turn the information into tips that your customers and strategic business partners can use.

What does it take to create social media content that clicks with your fans?

- **Brainstorm a list of frequently asked questions (FAQs).** Write about what your customers and strategic business alliances frequently ask about. Content that answers FAQs will be of interest to the audience and less self-promotional.

- **Plan an editorial schedule.** How often will you post? I recommend posting at least once a week. In some industries, where the audience is more tech savvy, you may need to post more often. How often you post comes back to knowing your fan profile.

- **Link to other resources.** Embed links in your posts to other sites that offer valuable information. Curating other value-added content is a legitimate approach to social selling.

Delivering value as a selling tool is as much attitude and state of mind as it is a marketing technique. You can train your mind to become more aware of possible post topics. Content is everywhere around you from everyday interactions with others to lessons learned on the job. When you have a brainstorm for a new post topic, make sure you write it down or better yet, record a voice memo on your smartphone and email it to yourself. Whether you go low-tech or high-tech, get in the habit of recording your ideas before you forget them.

Content ideas in case you get stuck in a self-promotional rut:

- **Book, Podcast and TED Talk Recommendations:** The next time you read a book or hear a talk that your audience could benefit from, tell them what stood out to you in a post.

- **Feature Hashtagged Events:** Take part in regular hashtagged events like Twitter's #FollowFriday or Facebook's #Throwback

Thursday (#TBT). These events are popular and provide an opportunity for you to showcase your personality.

- **Help Your Followers Out:** Watch for questions or problems relating to your industry, and your company in particular. Answer questions in a friendly way. Save the sales discussion for another day.

- **Jokes and Lighthearted Posts:** Social media is "social" so once in a while, it's ok to post something a little more lighthearted than usual. Jokes and funny images are usually well received and tend to deliver increased engagement.

- **Cute Photos:** It's no secret that kittens are the number one way to get engagement on social media, but cute kids are a close second. Look for some sweet viral videos or memes and share them periodically to see if you can get a bump in likes, comments and shares (or retweets!).

- **Mention Thought Leaders in Your Industry:** Have you heard a great speaker at an industry conference? Share what you learned from them on social media, tag them, and remember to include the conference hashtag. Giving a shout-out helps you build a strong network of contacts while adding value to your audience.

- **Outtakes and Mistakes:** Ever hit publish on a blog post and discover you made a major spelling error? Before you go and

correct it, take a screen grab and publish it on Facebook! Don't do this every time, but it's ok to show your human side from time to time and demonstrate your commitment to quality!

- **Ultimate Resource Lists:** Have you ever published a list-type article on your blog? You could do a shorter version and put it on your social media channels. Keep the list focused and, if possible, tag anyone you mention, such as authors or bloggers. They may decide to comment, like or share your post as a thank you!

- **Weekly Themed Posts:** One way to make your social media marketing strategy more effective is to come up with some weekly patterns for different types of content. For example, you might want to post an inspiring quote on Monday (Tip: label it #MotivationalMonday), share an industry post on Wednesday, and a tip of the week on Friday.

- **X vs. Y:** One effective way to boost engagement and encourage comments is to ask your followers to choose X vs. Y—such as, do you prefer burgers or hot dogs? If you're designing a new logo or product packaging, solicit opinions from your followers by posting images and asking which they prefer.

- **Questions for Followers:** Curious to know what your audience is thinking about? Ask! Twitter recently added a polling feature that lets your followers choose between two answers.

And you can ask questions directly in a status update on Facebook, Google+ or LinkedIn.

STRATEGY #3—BUILD A RELATIONSHIP

If you aren't sure how to maintain a positive relationship in the online world, think about what makes a good relationship in the offline world.

- Complete trust
- Open communication
- Mutual respect
- Quality time
- Thoughtful consideration
- Consistent commitment
- True loyalty
- Proactive problem solving
- Responsive dedication

Actions to help you build a solid relationship:

- **Post consistently.** Fans want to hear from you. Spend quality time "together" online. Don't disappear for weeks and then overpost to compensate. How often you should post depends on your fans' preferences and the social media channel's culture.

- **Communicate openly.** If a fan posts something negative, don't delete the post and act like it never happened. Respond

immediately with a next-action step to investigate the complaint and work toward a resolution.

- **Follow through.** If you say you will post new pictures soon, stick to your word. If you promise a coupon is coming soon, make it happen. If you promise a resolution to a complaint, make sure the issue is resolved.

- **Observe netiquette.** Respect your fans' privacy. Never, ever share their information with a third party, no matter how tempting.

- **Be authentic.** If your company doesn't really have a bounce house in the conference room, don't post that you do just to look more hip and trendy. Don't post fake testimonials and pose as customers.

- **Reciprocate kindness.** Do small things to thank your fans. Imagine how shocked a fan would be to receive a personal, handwritten thank-you note from your CEO or a phone call from the chairman of the board. Don't forget about low-tech, high-touch acts that would mean a lot to someone.

- **Connect with fans.** If your fans have similar business interests, introduce them to each other (with permission, of course).

- **Respond immediately.** Respond to all social media mentions, tags, comments, and shares. Show gratitude and thank others for their mentions. If someone asks a question or makes a comment, respond immediately. Speed is valued and appreciated.

STRATEGY #4—MASTER THE ART OF THE SHOUT OUT

I talked about this strategy extensively in *FANtastic Marketing*. One of the unintended consequences of social media is a meteoric rise in narcissism. With social media we have an outlet to share every aspect of our lives and some take it too far. Salespeople posting six to eight selfies per day definitely takes it too far!

Because of the incredible amount of self-indulgence online, content that shines the spotlight on others stands out and is highly memorable.

- **Thank Someone:** Spreading good cheer online is always a good idea, especially as a break from the negativity that seems to crop up so often on social media. If you experienced excellent customer service or someone helped you solve a problem, give them a public "thank you." It's a great way to let the world know how much you appreciated the service, and the company will appreciate the testimonial. Thank your vendor partners who help make you and your company successful. Thank your channel partners. Thank your team members in your company. Shine a light on others and it will come back to you tenfold.

- **Reply to Messages:** If your fans and followers take the time to comment on your Facebook page, or to send you a tweet, make sure you respond in a timely fashion. It shows you care and are responsive.

- **Share Other People's Updates:** Retweeting or sharing other people's content is a great way to show your audience that you respect opinions from other thought leaders in your industry and aren't focused entirely on yourself.

Being sociable on social media is a long-term business-building strategy. It will not produce leads and sales overnight. In addition, being social on social media in no way replaces networking and prospecting with phone calls, networking events, trade shows, and attending association events. However, what I have found is that it makes networking and prospecting easier. I rarely walk into a room of strangers. Thanks to my extensive social media presence, I have far-reaching connections that make it easy for me to strike up a conversation, build rapport, and find something or someone we have in common. I also find that when I meet my social media connections in person for the first time, we start our relationship on a deeper, more intimate level. They know all about my son and my fun-loving, sports-obsessed husband. They know I have two new books and they ask me for more information about them. Being sociable on social media is the ultimate icebreaker. And as a natural-born introvert, I can use all the ice breaking I can get.

FORMULATE YOUR GAME PLAN

Five FANtastic Questions to Help You Become More Sociable

- -

1. What social media channels are your fans using? How did you come to those conclusions?

_____

_____

_____

_____

_____

_____

_____

2. Are you consistently posting on social media? What percentage of your posts are sales versus non-sales messages?

_____

_____

_____

_____

_____

_____

_____

3. What is your favorite type of content on social media? What do you gravitate toward? How could you incorporate that type of content for your business?

_____

_____

_____

_____

_____

_____

_____

_____

4. What does "the art of the shout-out" mean to you? How could you use that on social media to build relationships with your fans?

_____

_____

_____

_____

_____

_____

_____

_____

5. Tweet me a shout-out @MeredithCSP with the #FANtasticSelling hashtag and I will tweet right back at you!

_____

_____

_____

_____

_____

_____

_____

_____

_____

ef·fi·cient

achieving maximum productivity with minimum
wasted effort or expense

Does using technology make you
feel 'appy or apprehensive?

WHAT DO SUCCESSFUL REAL ESTATE agents do differently
than those who are struggling? To what degree does technology
assist or hinder real estate agents from being successful? In 2011,
Active Rain conducted a survey of 1,758 real estate agents to find
out what separates the top professionals (those earning over
$100,000 a year, the 'Rich Real Estate Agents') from the strug-
gling professionals (those earning under $35,000 a year, the 'Poor
Real Estate Agents')[29]. Here's the rest of the story...

The Active Rain study concluded that rich real estate agents do in fact invest in and use technology, specifically CRM and email marketing, more heavily than poor agents.[30]

- Rich real estate agents invest six times more in technology.
- Rich real estate agents broadcast via social media.
- Rich real estate agents spend ten times more on marketing.
- Rich real estate agents are 87% more likely to use CRM to build a database of leads.
- Rich real estate agents are 54% more likely to use an email newsletter.
- Rich real estate agents are 35% more likely to blog and 78% more likely to use online video.

You may or may not be a real estate agent, but regardless of what type of sales position you hold, I think you can learn from the point I am making with the results of the Active Rain survey. **Your level of success as a salesperson is directly linked to your adoption and usage of technology tools.** In Chapter Seven, I referenced a 2016 LinkedIn Survey titled "State of Sales 2016." In addition to the findings regarding the importance of social selling tools, the survey also concluded the following:

What differentiates top salespeople and average performers? One of the key factors is their use of sales technology. Salespeople who have risen to the top of their field are frequent users of sales intelligence and social selling tools. Seventy-seven percent of top

salespeople rely on sales intelligence tools, compared with 52 percent of overall sales professionals.

Plus, top salespeople are 24 percent more likely to attribute their success to sales technology: 82 percent of top salespeople cite sales tools as "critical" to their ability to close deals, compared with 66 percent overall. They cite sales technology in general as key to their success, as well as specific tools. 76 percent of top sales performers cite social selling tools as "critical" or "extremely critical" to their ability to close deals.[31]

What does technology do for a salesperson? Technology tools automate time-wasting tasks. Technology tools help you communicate more effectively. Technology tools help you build and nurture relationships. Technology tools help you assess your effectiveness by measuring your efforts. Technology tools give you a competitive advantage by providing your fan's insight and analysis into their business. In this chapter I am going to focus on using technology tools to automate tasks and become more efficient. Salespeople have so many demands on their time from conference calls, to sales reports, to researching the competition, that often there is little or no time left for actual sales-related activities such as lead nurturing, prospecting, and networking. Efficient sales people stay focused on sales activities because they use technology tools to automate as many of the mundane, routine, non-sales related activities as possible. **The eighth trait of a rock-star, quota-busting, top-producing salesperson is the ability to be efficient.**

I know what you are thinking...*using technology takes me longer and slows me down.* It does that to everyone at first. You will have to invest additional time to become more proficient with your CRM and smartphone or tablet. At first it will take you longer to use technology than your old analog way of doing things. But in the long run, with practice and patience, there is no question that using technology to become more efficient will pay off. One of my favorite quotes is "Life begins at the end of your comfort zone." For some of you, your comfort zone consists of your legal pad, daytimer, and rolodex. I am living proof that once you step outside of your technology comfort zone you will reap major rewards in your career. And, if this chapter completely overwhelms you and makes you feel like a dinosaur—take a deep breath and keep reading. In Chapter Nine we are going to cover both free and paid resources to get you the training you need to be effective with technology tools.

WHAT'S 'APPENING

In this chapter I am going to recommend a series of apps to help you become more efficient. Your smartphone and/or tablet is a true sales power tool. How effectively are you using it to help you to be more efficient, organized, productive, and accessible to your fans?

A great app should solve a problem. Think of an app as a tool that automates mundane, time sucking, routine tasks. I believe technology should make our lives easier. I don't believe in using technology for the cool factor or because everyone else is using it at the moment. If it doesn't actually improve my life and give me more time for the people and things I love most, then I'm not interested. So it's from that perspective that I make the recommendations below.

Most of the apps I am recommending are available for both iOS and Android users, and most have both free versions and paid versions. I will indicate when I recommend that you upgrade to the paid version. I personally use all of these apps on a regular basis so I am confident that they work well. However, if you investigate one of these apps, and it seems hard to use or doesn't work with your other technology or business model, just search the app store for an alternative and you will find dozens of other options. Just because I find an app easy to use doesn't mean you will and that's okay. I find that many technology users (particularly older generations) blame themselves rather than blaming the faulty technology. Don't blame yourself or assume it's your fault if a computer or app doesn't work for you. Stop apologizing! Good technology should be one-click easy to use, no matter the skill level. If the technology isn't one-click easy for you, don't take the blame; just move-on and find a better solution.

TECHNOLOGY HARDWARE

I am an unapologetic fan of everything Apple. I'm somewhat embarrassed to admit our household of three people owns eight Apple devices (1 Mac, 3 iPhones, 3 iPads, and 1 Apple Watch). Two years ago I finally converted from a PC to a Mac computer. I had always assumed it would be hard to learn how to use a Mac because PCs and Macs operate so differently and none of my old files would be accessible on the new computer. Both of those assumptions proved to be completely false. I love my Mac and will never go back! Yes, Apple products are more expensive than their competitors, but there is a good reason for that. In this case the old adage "you get what you pay for" is 100% correct. There are more apps available for Apple devices compared to Android. Apple products are incredibly intuitive and easy to use, and the customer service and support is unmatched. You may not have control over what devices you use at work, but if you have input or need new devices for home, Apple products are the way to go.

PRODUCTIVITY APPS

Your number one productivity app is your CRM software. I've already hammered on the importance of using your CRM in Chapter Six so I won't get on that soapbox again. If any of the apps below complicate the use of your CRM or duplicate the functionality of your CRM, you should always use the functionality within the CRM over an outside app. If you don't have a CRM, or your CRM doesn't have the functionality listed below, or if you need help being more productive in your personal life, then the list below is meant to help conquer mundane, routine, time-sucking tasks faster and more efficiently.

- **Nozbe.** This is my favorite task management, to-do app of all time. I've tried so many and found most of them took more than they actually helped me. This app has a very simple user interface. Thanks to this app, I am finally remembering all of my to-dos and getting them done on time (or even early). You can try it free for 30 days and after that there are plans ranging from free to paid versions. It is worth every penny and more!

- **DocuSign.** Access, sign and send important documents from your desk, on the road and everywhere in between. No more waiting until you get back to your office to execute a contract. DocuSign works with the services, applications, and devices you already use: Microsoft, Salesforce, Google, Apple and many more. Free 30-day trial.

- **Cam Scanner.** Convert paper documents into digital versions and save them to your mobile phone or computer. Just take a photo and Cam Scanner digitizes the document. You can batch scan multi-page documents. Create PDFs or JPEG files. Free and paid versions.

- **CamCard.** Admit it, you have a drawer full of business cards from networking events that never made it into your contacts. I know this because I'm guilty too! With CamCard, you can scan, manage, sync, and exchange business cards. CamCard integrates with the Salesforce.com CRM. Free and paid versions.

- **LogMeIn.** With this app you can access your computer from any device. No more waiting until you get back to your computer to accomplish a simple task. Store, share, and collaborate on files in one click. Print remote documents to a local printer. Free 30-day trial.

- **MileBug.** Track miles and expenses for every trip right on your phone. You can set-up frequent destinations. Export mileage reports in either HTML or CSV format. Free and paid versions.

- **LastPass.** Do you have trouble remembering all of your online usernames and passwords? I do! I used to waste so much time trying to log in to my online accounts. LastPass securely remembers all of your online passwords each time you log in to a site for the first time. The next time you log in to that site, LastPass remembers the password and logs in for you. Once LastPass is set-up you only need to remember one master password. Free and paid versions. I absolutely recommend the paid version of this app because of the sensitive nature of the information it is storing.

- **MobileDay.** I love the tagline on the homepage of MobileDay's website, "Give dialing the finger." That's funny! The MobileDay app syncs with your smartphone, notifies you of your upcoming meeting, and connects you to the conference call with one touch. No more writing down the conference call number and password on a napkin as you frantically try to log in on time. As long as the conference call number and password are in your calendar, you are good to go. And, even better, this app is free!

ORGANIZATION APPS

The apps in this list are meant to help you stay organized. From file management to note taking, it can be difficult to keep all of your paper and digital files organized and accessible. Searching for files or trying to share files with others is a huge timewaster. These apps will eliminate those frustrations.

- **Dropbox.** Known to most professionals, Dropbox is a cloud-based file storage service that makes it easy to send, receive, and share files. No more waiting until you get back to the office to retrieve a document from your hard drive or snail mailing someone a USB drive to share a file. With Dropbox, you can have remote access to all of your files and easily share files that are too large to email. Free and paid versions.

- **ShareFile.** For some clients, the use of Dropbox presents challenges. Some do not use the service so they don't have a login or they struggle with finding the files needed inside another user's Dropbox account. When that happens, I use ShareFile by Citrix. It is more intuitive than Dropbox and super easy to use. Some of our internal team members actually prefer it over Dropbox. ShareFile is a paid service.

- **Google Drive.** Google Drive allows you to create, manage, share and collaborate on files such as documents and spread-sheets. With a Google Doc multiple people can work on the same document and not save over each other's work. The documents are stored in the cloud and accessible from any device with internet access. Completely free to use.

- **Evernote.** I love taking handwritten notes, but with my travel schedule, it isn't practical to have all of my paper notebooks with me. Evernote allows me to take notes, organize them into folders with tags, and have access to them from any of my devices year round, day and night. Google Chrome has an awesome extension for Evernote that allows you to clip articles, pages, bookmarks, and PDFs from the web. The Evernote extension strips out all of the extraneous graphics on the page and then saves them to my Evernote account. I use Evernote so often that it was worth upgrading to the paid version.

- **Smartsheet.** If you need to manage projects, I highly recommend Smartsheet. I've used a number of project management tools such as BaseCamp and found they caused me more work than time saved. So I went back to a Google Doc spreadsheet, but that proved too basic. One day, on a whim, I googled *spreadsheet on steroids* and the Smartsheet app popped up. Smartsheet is a project management and collaboration tool that has streamlined the look of a simple spreadsheet and merged it with the functionality of project management software. Paid versions only.

- **Slack.** This is the newest tool in my arsenal and has been a total game changer. If you are drowning in email from your co-workers, Slack is the answer. Think of it as instant

messaging, email, file sharing, and to-do list management for teams all rolled into one tool. Free and paid versions.

SOCIAL MEDIA MANAGEMENT APPS

You need the right tools to successfully execute the social selling ideas I shared with you in Chapter Seven. These apps will help you automate and consolidate your social media marketing efforts.

- **Hootsuite.** I use Hootsuite to write and schedule my pre-scheduled social media posts. I love being able to go to one place to write a week's worth of posts in one sitting and schedule them from one account. Hootsuite is also my favorite way to monitor Twitter mentions and retweets from my desktop computer. Hootsuite will also allow you to monitor other sites like Facebook, LinkedIn and Instagram, but I primarily use it to monitor Twitter. Free and paid versions.

- **Facebook, Instagram, LinkedIn, and Twitter.** You can absolutely monitor all of these in Hootsuite, but honestly, I prefer to use the native app on my smartphone or tablet for spontaneous posts and interacting with other's posts. Free to use.

- **Sprout Social.** I primarily use Sprout Social, social media management software, for the reporting function. Clean, attractive and easy to read, Sprout Social reports can be customized to display your company's logo. The Sprout Social reports also provide a nice summary of the analytics for each of your social media pages. Paid version only.

GREETING CARD AND POSTCARD APPS

All of the apps in this list allow you to send customized, personalized postcards and/or greeting cards from your smartphone or tablet. If you want to WOW your fans, send them something in the mail! We rely so heavily on digital forms of communication that good old-fashioned snail mail really stands out and says that you care. I love to send greeting cards, but I have trouble getting to the drugstore to buy one and then getting to the mailbox to mail them. Good news! There's an app for that! Problem solved. Now I can send high-touch greeting cards using high-tech apps. The cards cost less than a greeting card from the store (postage included) and they are completely personalized. You simply create the card on your smartphone or tablet, click send, and the app does the printing and mailing for you. Amazing!

- **Ink.** This is my favorite app on the relationship app list. It is incredibly easy to use. They have hundreds of greeting card templates to choose from and you can easily add a custom photo and message to the template. I prefer to use my tablet to create the cards because I can proof them more effectively with a larger screen. I like the style of the cards and the messages they use.

- **Just Wink.** Looking for a fun, off-beat, slightly irreverent card that will be highly memorable? Send them a Just Wink card. You can personalize the cards with your own messages and photos.

- **Red Stamp.** With this app you can create custom digital and paper greeting cards. Red Stamp also has a nice selection of invitations and announcements. It is similar to the Ink Cards app, but the style of the cards are different, so it depends on personal preference which one you use.

- **Paperless Post.** This app combines greeting cards (both digital and paper) with online event invitations (think Evite). You can order business holiday cards and gifts from the website.

- **Pixinote.** This app creates a one-sided postcard that you add a photo and a message to. It is mailed in a fun brown paper envelope that has a unique design and shape. This app is super fast and easy to use because the design time is minimal. This is an easy way to send a personalized, quick *thank you* or *thinking of you* type of message.

- **Felt.** Do you like the idea of sending cards from your smartphone, but miss the look and feel of a handwritten card? Welcome to Felt! Write the greeting on your smartphone screen using your finger or a stylus and the Felt app pulls the text into the card. All of the cards are square and you can use up to four personalized photos per card. Cards are mailed within 24 hours and even the envelope can be handwritten. These cards are the most expensive of the group but the look and feel is so unique that it is worth it.

MARKETING, PHOTOGRAPHY & GRAPHIC DESIGN APPS

I am not a properly trained graphic designer. I do not know how to use Photoshop or InDesign. But on occasion I find that I need to be able to quickly and easily create my own graphics for social media and event marketing. The following apps will help you enhance your photos and create simple graphics. If I can use them, so can you!

- **Pic Stitch.** This allows you to easily edit and frame multiple photos into one photo collage. You can export images to Facebook, Twitter, Instagram and more. Free to use.

- **Over.** This fast and easy photo editor allows you to easily add text to your photos. It has more than 10,000+ graphics and fonts available. Free to use.

- **Aviary.** If I'm editing photos on my phone or tablet and I don't want to add text to them, I use Aviary. I can crop, adjust, and add filters as needed. There are tools for text, special effects, frames, and stickers. I can whiten teeth, eliminate red eye, and remove blemishes. Free to use.

- **Fotor.** If I'm editing photos on my desktop, then I use Fotor. This program is a great photo editor that allows me to resize, edit, and crop my photos. I can add effects, borders, and text. Free to use

-

- **WordSwag.** This app is similar to Over in that you can use it to add words to your photos. It will also create stylish graphics from a quote or catchphrase. Easily share designs on Instagram, Facebook, Pinterest, Twitter, and Tumblr. Thousands of free image backgrounds and fonts are available. Paid version only.

- **Photofy.** Similar to Over and WordSwag, Photofy allows you to add words and graphics to your photos. But it does so much more than that! Photofy has thousands of free and paid templates that you can place photos into to turn your ordinary photo into an online birthday card or holiday greeting. Free and paid versions.

- **Canva.** I cannot say enough good things about Canva. Available on your desktop, tablet and phone, Canva allows you to create professional-looking graphics like Facebook images and Twitter ads with a super easy drag-and-drop interface. From social media graphics to presentations, there really isn't anything you can't design in Canva using a template or starting from scratch. Free to use as an individual, paid version for teams.

- **Snagit.** I probably use Snagit no less than 15 to 20 times per day! Snagit is an easy screen-capture tool. I also use it to open images for cropping and resizing. Paid version only. Totally worth every penny!

BONUS! MY FAVORITE LIFESTYLE APPS

These apps may or may not help you make more sales, but they will make your life easier and more fun so I couldn't help but include them. Have fun with them and enjoy!

- **Instabeauty.** Do you ever wonder how celebrities manage to look so good in their selfies? They use Instabeauty! This app edits your selfies to make you look like a movie star. It whitens teeth, removes blemishes, and even makes your face thinner. It's like Photoshop Botox for your selfies without the actual Photoshop or Botox. Free to use.

- **Pinterest.** Known as the world's catalog of ideas, Pinterest allows users to browse millions of virtual how-to pins such as how to style an outfit, how to clean stubborn grout stains in the bathroom, or how to bake a perfect Minecraft birthday cake for your eight-year-old son. No matter what task you want to accomplish, you can search for it on Pinterest and there will be a pin with ideas and instructions on how to complete that task. Users create virtual pin boards with ideas organized by category so you can easily find your favorite ideas at a later time. Warning: Pinterest is an addiction. Proceed at your own risk! Free to use.

- **RetailMeNot.** I don't have time to clip coupons and when I do I typically forget to take them with me to the store. The RetailMeNot app has digital coupons eliminating the need for paper coupons completely. Search by retailer name or

via a map of stores near your location. The app shows you both in-store and online coupons for the retailer of interest. When you check out, the cashier simply scans the coupon from your phone and you save money. Free to use.

- **Cartwheel.** This is the coupon app solely for Target shoppers. You can scan items as you shop and the app will tell you if additional savings are available. Save the digital coupons to your account and when you check out, the cashier scans your phone to deduct the savings from your total. Free to use.

- **eBates.** Save money while you shop for items you planned to buy anyway. Simply browse the app for your online retailer of choice. Click on the retailer's link from the eBates website or app, go shopping on the retailer's website, and once a quarter you will receive a check from eBates. Rebates range from 1% to 10% per store and change daily. The eBates rebate percentage is in addition to whatever sales and coupons the retailer is offering. It's a deal! Free to use.

- **WhiteNoise.** I use this app every single night to create white noise so I can sleep undisturbed. I used to use a small white noise machine to block out noise both at home and at hotels. Now I don't need that extra device. Choose from dozens of white noise sounds and enjoy a wonderful night's sleep. Free and paid versions. I actually like the white noise selections in the free version better than the paid version.

- **Mezi.** Wish you had a personal assistant? Meet Mezi, your smartphone virtual personal shopping assistant. Tell Mezi what you need—from travel plans to shopping needs—and Mezi will search the web for you and present a series of options for you review. It's like having a personal shopper and travel agent right on your smartphone. Free to use.

- **eMeals.** I am a horrible cook. Yet several nights a week I need to produce healthy and delicious meals for my family. Before eMeals, I spent a lot of time food shopping and cooking. For a nominal annual fee, once a week eMeals emails me a seven-day meal plan that includes a grocery shopping list for all of the items needed for the recipes (the meal plan is also sent to my eMeals app on my phone and tablet). You can choose from a variety of meal plan types from Low Fat to Vegetarian to Paleo. I take the eMeals shopping list, go to my grocery's online ordering website, order my food online, wait for confirmation, then pull up to the front door of the grocery and they load the groceries into my car. I never even go into the store! That's a major time saver. Paid version only. Totally worth it for us non-cooks!

- **TripIt.** I saved the best app for last! With TripIt, all of your travel confirmations are saved into one itinerary within the app. No more printing out your hotel reservation confirmation and digging through your backpack looking for the piece of paper or scrolling through piles of emails looking for the flight departure time. Simply forward your travel confirmations to plans@tripit.com and the app imports all of the information into one itinerary. The app links to Google maps for directions and also tracks your travel reward account balances. This app has a free version, but if you travel enough the paid version is well worth it. The paid version tracks the price of your airline ticket and if the ticket goes on sale the app alerts you so you can get a refund from the airline. Free and paid version.

Wow! That's a lot of apps! You may not need all of these apps and some of them you may not find useful. Again, that's okay. **What are some of the mundane, manual tasks throughout your day that keep you from focusing on sales activities?** The goal of this chapter is to help you identify those tasks and inspire you to look for a technology solution. Once you identify what tasks you need help automating or outsourcing, go the app store of your choice and do a search for apps to solve that particular problem. Look through the choices carefully and pay attention to the reviews. Review the list of features and screenshots of the app to determine if it really does what you need it to do. If there is a free version of an app, try the free version first to see if you really find it useful before you spend money on the paid version. Don't forget to periodically delete apps from your smartphone or tablet that you are not using or you will develop a storage problem.

If the app looks complicated or doesn't meet your needs, remember, don't blame yourself for a lack of technological prowess. Simply move on and shake off the technology shame! Look for apps that make sense to you and fit your needs. Everything else is just white noise and it doesn't mean you aren't cool, hip, or relevant. At the same time, don't be afraid to try something new just because you didn't grow up using technology. I've worked with plenty of millennial-aged clients who were less tech savvy than I am. Age and experience have nothing to do with using technology. Like most things, your patience level, attitude, and commitment to learning are far more important. Now get your phone out and let's get 'appening!

FORMULATE YOUR GAME PLAN

Five FANtastic Questions to Help You Become More Efficient

- -

1. What percentage of your day is spent on sales activities (lead nurturing, prospecting, networking) versus non-sales activities (administrative tasks, meetings, and emails)?

2. What is one action you could take today to spend more time on sales activities (without neglecting your other work)? When will you take that action?

3. On a scale from 1 to 5 (5 being a technology Jedi Master and 1 being a caveman trying to learn how to start a fire with flint), how comfortable are you with technology, your CRM, your smartphone, and apps?

_____

_____

_____

_____

_____

_____

_____

4. If you scored a 1 to 3 on Question #3, what is one action you need to take to become a solid 4 or 5 on the technology comfort and usage rating scale? When will you take that action?

_____

_____

_____

_____

_____

_____

_____

5. Send me an email at meredith@creatingwow.com with your favorite app and why. I would love to hear from you what apps make a difference in your professional or personal life.

pre·pared

properly expectant, organized, or equipped; ready

Do you know what you don't know?

I STARED AT THE COMPUTER screen. I had a decision to make. Give up and quit or keep going. In that moment, I realized the laptop computer in front of me was standing between me and my future. Here's the rest of the story...

On my first day of graduate school at Rollins College, I was issued a laptop computer. I had no idea how to use it. My employer at the time had a mainframe system with proprietary software and I had never used a personal computer before or any of the Microsoft suite of programs like Word or Excel (okay now I just sound old!). Here's the rub...I had just enrolled in a $40,000 Master's Degree in Corporate Communication and Technology and the laptop was issued as part of the program and I was expected to use it. I spent the first weekend unable to find any of the files I saved to the hard drive during class. I told my husband that I was going to have to quit the program. Ever the steady one, my husband stuck a Post-It Note® to my computer that read: *A = Floppy Disk* and *C = Hard Drive*. He explained the difference and helped me find my files. With his encouragement, I decided to keep going. I had no idea how I would keep from failing out of the program, but I knew I had to take the first step and catch up with the rest of the world.

Maybe you are feeling the same way right now. Maybe you struggle using social media, your smartphone, or CRM. Or perhaps you are a technology native and you struggle with some of the other traits, such as being sociable, engaging, and/or inquisitive. Whatever your professional challenges, let me assure you that you are not alone. No one is good at everything. The difference between rock-star salespeople and mediocre salespeople is the willingness to learn, change, and grow. I am here to encourage you and give you the resources you need to be successful. It's my way of paying forward what my husband did for me (and still does every single day).

The ninth undeniable trait of a rock-star, top-producing, quota-busting, FANtastic salesperson is the ability to be prepared. Being prepared means you have a wide and deep knowledge of your product, your fans, and your competition. Nothing less is effective when you are selling to internet-empowered customers. How prepared are you to engage with a customer who has an unlimited amount of information at their fingertips?

Being prepared also means you are willing to learn. There are two areas that you must commit to learning more about: 1) The skills, attitudes, and behaviors that you are *lacking* so you can manage those weaknesses effectively, and 2) The skills, attitudes, and behaviors that are your *strengths* so you can enhance and improve your natural-born gifts.

In Chapter Eight, I mentioned Marcus Buckingham's book, *Now, Discover Your Strengths*, and I absolutely believe in the premise of the book. The more you operate from your strengths, the more successful you will be. However, I also believe you must expose yourself to knowledge outside your strength zone so you can effectively manage and mitigate your weaknesses. It's just like our moms always tried to tell us about a new food, *how do you know you don't like it until you try it?* How do you know you are not good at technology or being sociable on social media until you learn more about it?

What if you discover you are better at a skill or behavior than you originally thought? Are you mentally prepared to change, grow, and learn new things? Are you open to the idea that you might not have all the necessary knowledge, and are you willing to do something about it? Do you know where to access the knowledge you are lacking? You must be willing to admit, "I am not as prepared as I should be and it is hurting my career."

Many years ago my mom gave me some invaluable advice regarding finding a mate and it absolutely applies to this context as well. She told me to find someone who was willing to change and grow with me over the course of our lives together. She told me that over the course of a lifetime you inevitably change and that you need someone who can change and grow with you or you will find yourselves growing apart. Are you a person that expects to change and grow over the course of your career? Are you actively seeking those opportunities?

MAKE A COMMITMENT TO LIFELONG LEARNING

FANtastic salespeople prepare themselves for success with a commitment to lifelong learning. They are hungry for new information and skills and actively seek out learning opportunities. The Pew Research Center conducted a survey of 2,752 adults living in the United States and asked about the impact of lifelong learning activities[32]. Sadly, the study found that only 36% of all adults are professional learners, meaning they have taken a course or gotten additional training to improve job skills or expertise connected to career advancement. Of the respondents who had pursued professional learning opportunities, they stated the following benefits:

- 65% say their learning in the past 12 months expanded their professional network.
- 47% say their extra training helped them advance within their current company.
- 29% say it enabled them to find a new job with their current employer or a new one.
- 27% say it helped them consider a different career path.

The study also found a correlation between household income levels and lifelong learning. Some 83% of those living in households earning more than $75,000 are personal learners (studying for personal interest and betterment), compared with 65% of those living in households earning under $30,000. Similarly, 69% of workers living in households earning more than $75,000 are professional learners, compared with 49% of workers living in households earning under $30,000.

THREE TYPES OF LEARNING

Brian Tracy, an international sales training author, speaker, and consultant, recommends salespeople acquire three types of learning[33].

1. **Maintenance Learning**—This is the type of learning that keeps you current with your industry, your field, your company, and your products. Maintenance learning does not add to your current knowledge base. It simply helps you remain accurate and informed.

2. **Growth Learning**—This type of learning adds to your knowledge and skill set. This type of learning exposes you to new ideas that you were not aware of. Growth learning opportunities are all around you. I am going to share many growth learning resources in this chapter.

3. **Shock Learning**—This type of learning contradicts a piece of knowledge or understanding that you already have. Shock learning comes with experience when something happens that causes you to question your existing assumptions.

INVEST IN YOURSELF

Top-producing, quota-busting sales professionals invest in learning opportunities and technology tools. Salespeople frequently tell me the reason they are not attending a training class or using a tablet during the sales process is because their employer won't pay for it. That is an excuse, not a reason. Being prepared means spending your own time and money learning new skills, behaviors, and knowledge. It also means investing in your own tools. The Active Rain study mentioned in Chapter Eight found:

> *Rich Agents invest 6 times as much in technology as poor real estate agents. Every year the average rich real estate agent spends $3,000-5,000 per year on technology, while the poor real estate agent only spends $500-1,000 per year. So, for every one dollar that the poor agent spends on technology, the rich agent spends six dollars. Think about this: the average rich real estate agent spends more money in a month, than some poor real estate agents spend on technology all year.*

Create an annual Personal Development Budget (PDB) for your personal and professional learning needs. How much you spend is completely up to you. You may want to set aside a percentage of your commission or percentage of your annual income. The important thing is that you write down an amount you are willing to invest and you take action on that commitment.

For some of you the issue is not spending money, it's about taking the time to attend a training class or read a new book. You are busy and successful and there isn't any extra time for learning new things. This approach will work in the short-term, but in the long-term you will burn out. You will "hit the wall" mentally and physically unless you start feeding your brain and your soul with nourishing knowledge and peer interaction. You may also find yourself less relevant over time if you are not investing in the maintenance and growth type of learning that Brian Tracy recommended above.

ONLINE LEARNING RESOURCES

The Pew Research Center study I mentioned earlier also found that most learners prefer an in person learning experience versus an online learning experience. In addition, the study revealed an overall lack of knowledge of online learning resources. In this next section, I am going to highlight some of my favorite online learning resources and, in the following section, discuss some of my favorite in person learning resources. Please do not make the mistake of assuming you can't learn from an online resource. Videos, webinars, Twitter chats, and online courses are all excellent sources of knowledge and are generally cost-effective to use. How do you know you can't learn from an online course until you try it? If you tried one and didn't find it to be helpful, consider that the problem may have been that particular course and not the learning method itself.

1. **YouTube.** You can learn how to do just about anything by watching videos on YouTube. The day after I purchased my first Mac computer, I went to YouTube and simply typed in "how to use a Mac." I found a one-hour free tutorial that

taught me all of the basics. Within the hour I was up and running on the new computer.

2. **Lynda.com.** Lynda.com is the leading online learning website with more than 4,000 courses in business, technology, and creative skills taught by industry experts. Learn how to use software like Microsoft Word, PowerPoint and/or Excel. You can learn how to create presentations, how to use social media, and even soft skills like productivity, communication, and leadership. The site offers a free trial and low-cost monthly subscription plans. If you don't see courses that interest you on Lynda.com, simply Google "online courses like Lynda.com" and a number of other sites come up. Udemy, Skillshare, and Coursera are just a few of the other options available.

3. **Podcasts.** I am a news/talk-radio junkie. I could listen to talk radio all day, analyzing political campaigns, local, and national news. But I found that when I listened to that all day I became stressed and negative. I've replaced news/talk radio with podcasts, and the change in my attitude, outlook, and energy level is amazing. A simple Google search for "top sales podcasts" will reveal hundreds of options. Start using your commute time or exercise time to listen to podcasts. Ranging from free to low cost, podcasts are an excellent way to obtain growth learning.

HIGHLY RATED SALES PODCASTS:

- The Ultimate Sales Hustle, Steli Efti of Close.io
- B2B Growth Show, James Carbary of Sweet Fish Media
- The Sales Blog—In The Arena, Anthony Iannarino
- Salesman Podcast, Will Barron of Salesman.Red
- The Sales Evangelist, Donald Kelly
- Accelerate!, Andy Paul
- The Social Selling Podcast, Greg, Martin & Elyse of Linking into Sales
- The Brutal Truth About Sales and Selling, Brian Burns

HIGHLY RATED PERSONAL AND PROFESSIONAL DEVELOPMENT PODCASTS:

- The Kickass Life, David Wood
- Let It Out, Katie Dalebout
- Read to Lead, Jeff Brown
- School of Greatness, Lewis House
- Profit. Power. Pursuit., Tara Gentile
- The Tim Ferriss Show, Tim Ferriss
- This Is Your Life, Michael Hyatt

4. **TED Talks.** If you aren't familiar with TED, it is a nonprofit devoted to the spread of new ideas. TED began in 1984 as a conference featuring TED talks, 18-minute powerful talks focused on Technology, Entertainment, and Design. Today, TED talks cover a wide variety of topics from science to social issues. You can access the TED talks on your desktop computer via the TED.com website or on your tablet or smartphone using the TED app. TED talks are a FANtastic

way to obtain growth and shock learning. Thousands of speakers apply to speak at the TED conference each year and only a few are selected, so the quality of the information and ideas being presented are without compare. The TED conference became so popular it spawned regional TEDx events. If you learn that a TEDx event is being hosted in your area, plan to attend. TEDx events showcase new ideas from the best of the best in your local area.

I love TED talks because they are short and pack a lot of information into one 18-minute segment. I also love them because the focus is on new ideas and most of the talks use in-depth research to back their claims.

Attach.io recommends the following 12 TED Talks as must-see for every salesperson:

1. Are We in Control of Our Decisions, Dan Ariely
2. The Puzzle of Motivation, Dan Pink
3. The Walk from "No" to "Yes", William Ury
4. Life Lessons From an Ad Man, Rory Sutherland
5. Simplicity Sells, David Pogue
6. The Science of Sales, Donald Doane
7. A Sale Is a Love Affair, Jack Vincent
8. What's Next in Sales, Wes Schaeffer
9. Your Body Language Shapes Who You Are, Amy Cuddy
10. The Psychology of Your Future Self, Dan Gilbert
11. How to Make Stress Your Friend, Kelly McGonigal
12. How to Make Work-Life Balance Work, Nigel Marsh

CLASSROOM AND IN-PERSON LEARNING OPPORTUNITIES

1. **Apple Workshops and Genius Bar.** Need help transforming your smartphone or tablet into a sales power tool? If you have an Apple device be sure to take advantage of their free support advisors called the Genius Bar and their free workshops. The free hour-long workshops will not only teach you how to use your Apple devices more effectively, but they cover broader topics, such as creating presentations. Apple even offers a summer camp program for kids that is made up of three sessions where kids learn movie making, robotics, coding, and storytelling.

LEARN HOW TO USE YOUR DEVICES MORE EFFICIENTLY AND EFFECTIVELY:

- Apple Watch
- Apple TV
- iPad
- Mac
- iPhone
- iPod

LEARN HOW TO UTILIZE APPLE PRODUCTS AND SERVICES:

- iTunes
- Apple Music
- iCloud

LEARN TECHNOLOGY SKILLS SUCH AS:

- Photography
- Videography
- Presentations

My understanding is that Microsoft has a similar service to the Apple Genius Bar called the Answer Desk. I can't vouch for it because I haven't used it personally, but if you are a Microsoft user look into that for similar types of support.

2. **Association Conferences, Workshops, Seminars, and Networking.** Become a member of your industry association and start actively attending the association's conferences, workshops, seminars, and educational networking meetings. In my opinion, you are not serious about your career if you do not support your local industry association by being a member and attending events. Your local association exists to serve and protect the industry. The least you can do is support their efforts. If your employer will not pay for membership, then include the annual fee in your personal development budget. Membership in your industry association will ensure you hit your maintenance learning objectives.

3. **Continuing Education (CE) Courses.** I am an approved instructor for a number of sales and marketing continuing education courses in the home building industry. It never fails to amaze me how poor the attendance is for those

courses. Education offered by your industry association is one of the most affordable education opportunities available. It is also guaranteed to be directly applicable to your job and it offers many indirect benefits, such as networking, relationship building, and career advancement. If you have a professional license that requires a certain number of CE hours per year, then you are taking advantage of these courses. But for those of you who do not have CE requirements, I urge you to set your own personal CE requirements and start taking advantage of these courses to fulfill your maintenance learning needs.

4. **Professional Designations.** Beyond continuing education courses, you should also pursue the professional designations and certifications available in your industry. Examples of professional designations include CSP (Certified Sales Professional) and CSE (Certified Sales Executive). Professional designations give you credibility with your fans. It is a third-party endorsement of your skills. It assures your fans that you are qualified to assist them. Professional certifications are also helpful when you are looking for a new sales position. It says to your (potential) employer that you are serious about your career and willing to invest time and money improving yourself.

5. **Mastermind Groups.** Find three to five likeminded sales professionals who do not compete with your products and services and form a mastermind group. Set a meeting

schedule and commit to attending. A mastermind group serves as your own personal board of directors. They can help you brainstorm solutions to challenges, serve as a resource, and offer support during difficult personal and professional seasons.

I hope you will take this chapter to heart and act on these ideas. My commitment to lifelong learning has served me well and I know it will help you too. Motivational guru Tony Robbins says, "The path to success is to take massive, determined action." Robbins defines massive action as the pursuit of a goal with deliberate steps. You simply cannot be the best of the best, blow past your sales goals, and build the lifestyle you desire without a commitment to lifelong learning. It won't happen. You might exist and eek out a good living, but without lifelong learning you will always be dependent on others and outside conditions for your success. Make the commitment today to take your success and family's future into your own hands. Do you know what you don't know? And, most importantly, what are you willing to do about it?

FORMULATE YOUR GAME PLAN

Five FANtastic Questions to Help You Become More Prepared

- -

1. Make a list of three skills, attitudes, or behaviors that you need to learn more about.

_____

_____

_____

_____

_____

_____

_____

2. What is one action you could take to learn more about the three items you listed in Question #1?

_____

_____

_____

_____

_____

_____

_____

3. Determine your PDB, Personal Development Budget, number. What is that number based on? How will you ensure that money is available to you throughout the year and doesn't get spent elsewhere?

_____

_____

_____

_____

_____

_____

_____

4. Are you a member of your local industry association? If not, research local associations and select one to join. Join in the next 30 days. If yes, what is the next educational event you could attend? Schedule that event on your calendar and get registered for it. No excuses!

_____

_____

_____

_____

_____

_____

_____

5. Send me an email at meredith@creatingwow.com with your favorite podcast or TED talk. I would love to hear what you listen to and watch to stay motivated.

_____

_____

_____

_____

_____

_____

_____

su·per·fan

a very or extremely devoted fan

Are you a Ritz Carlton or a
Red Roof Inn?

I LOOKED AT THE HOTEL checkout folio and gasped out loud. How did our free weekend at the Amelia Island Ritz Carlton Resort turn into a $2,000 weekend? Here's the rest of the story...

On our fifth wedding anniversary, Allen and I cashed in credit card points for a free weekend stay at the Amelia Island Ritz Carlton Resort. Upon our arrival, the valet opened my car door and said, "Welcome to the Ritz Carlton at Amelia Island. My name is Sam. And you are?" I enthusiastically told him my name and that we were celebrating our fifth wedding anniversary. He ushered us inside and walked us to the check-in desk. Sam introduced us to Maria, the check-in clerk. Maria greeted us with "Mr. and Mrs. Oliver, we've been expecting you! Welcome and Happy Anniversary!" She immediately handed us the room keys, a welcome packet, and introduced us to David, the bellman, to escort us to our room. She told David with great gusto, "Meet Mr. & Mrs. Oliver, they are from Orlando, Florida, and they are celebrating their fifth wedding anniversary."

David greeted us warmly, collected our luggage, and began to escort us to our room. He pointed out the entrance to the spa and mentioned several of their most popular treatments. He noticed my husband's golf clubs and described the resort golf course in great detail. He pointed out the pool, the resort restaurants, and made several local area recommendations.

When we arrived at the hotel room, he ushered us inside and proceeded to demonstrate the features and finishes of the hotel room. We stood in the bathroom as he pointed out the marble countertops, explained how to use the shower fixture, and discussed the merits of the giant soaker tub. He turned on the television and reviewed how to use the remote control. Last, but certainly not least, he threw back the curtains to the balcony with great flourish, slid open the glass sliding door, ushered us out onto the balcony and said with great enthusiasm "And, this is your view!"

Granted, it was a stunning, oceanfront view on a picture perfect spring day in Florida. But his unbridled enthusiasm was still quite remarkable. We walked back inside the room and that's when it happened. David lifted the phone from the cradle and dialed the spa. He looked at me and said, "Does 9 a.m. work for a deluxe package?" Hypnotized by the magic of the moment, I found myself automatically nodding yes. He looked at Allen and said, "While she is at the spa all morning, you might as well hit the links—tee time at 9 a.m. for you?" As he dialed the pro shop, Allen nodded yes. Lastly, he said, "And you certainly don't want to miss out on our Lobster Extravaganza tonight. You will dine by candlelight on the beach and it features lobster twenty-five ways." He dialed the dining reservation's extension and made a reservation for two. "Does 7 p.m. work?" We looked at each other, smiled, and nodded yes. How could we miss out on lobster twenty-five ways, on the ocean, by candlelight?

The entire FANtastic experience primed us to buy. From the initial warm greeting by the valet, to the personalized hand-off to the check-in clerk, to the exuberant resort tour by David, the bellman, clearly the Ritz Carlton has a sales process that is well defined and scripted. But just like the Pirates of the Caribbean ride at Disney World, the process was managed and handled with such finesse that I didn't once feel like I was on a pre-scripted ride being sold a bill of goods I didn't want.

As good as the sales process was, it would have been all for nothing without a FANtastic salesperson to make the sale. David was one of the most persuasive and effective salespeople I've ever met. He embodies all of the undeniable traits of a rock-star, top-producing, quota-busting, FANtastic salesperson described in the previous chapters.

1. **Relevant.** David only discussed features of the resort that matched our interests and hobbies.

2. **Insightful.** He shared knowledge about the resort, spa, and golf course that only an insider would know.

3. **Inquisitive.** David seemed genuinely interested in us as people and what we wanted to do at the resort that weekend.

4. **Engaging.** His enthusiasm and love for the resort was contagious.

5. **Authentic.** David's enthusiasm didn't seemed forced or canned.

6. **Nurturing.** He followed through and followed up throughout the stay to make sure we were having a wonderful time.

7. **Sociable.** David was friendly and warm throughout our entire stay.

8. **Efficient.** While he went into great detail on the resort tour and hotel room demonstration, it moved along quickly and didn't feel like it was taking too long.

9. **Prepared.** David had clearly practiced and rehearsed his lines. He knew how to precisely describe each resort feature, which benefits to highlight, how to demonstrate the room effectively, and when to go for the close.

It was a memorable, magical experience and as a result, I am a lifelong Ritz Carlton fan. I can't wait until my next, *ahem*, free weekend at a Ritz Carlton.

There is one more undeniable trait left to discuss and David at the Ritz Carlton exemplified it. **The tenth trait of a rock-star,**

top-producing, quota-busting FANtastic salesperson is the ability to be a superfan. When your fans know that you love them and that you care, they will be loyal no matter what. Of course, you can't break promise after promise and expect your fans to be loyal. But most mistakes and errors, handled properly, can be forgiven and forgotten, *if* they know you care. The question is, are you a superfan of your fans?

THE ULTIMATE SUPERFAN

Which scenario most resonates with you?

SCENARIO #1

You genuinely like your customers. They may irritate you from time to time, but for the most part, you enjoy interacting with them. You understand their unique challenges and look forward to being part of the solution. You think about them in your off time, brainstorming new ideas to help them be more successful.

SCENARIO #2

On Sunday evenings you are filled with dread at the thought of dealing with your customers on Monday. You often find yourself mentally rolling your eyes and shaking your head during meetings with your customers. You avoid phone calls and delete emails hoping to have as little interaction as possible.

If you have reached the point where Scenario #2 resonates with you more than Scenario #1, it is time to find a new job. It's time to change jerseys, so to speak, and move on. You will not achieve the sales results you or your boss desires if you are no longer a superfan of your fans. No matter how much you try to cover up your true feelings, your fans can sense the truth. Remember, your fans want authenticity from you and anything less will be rejected.

It's okay to admit you are no longer in love with your fans, as long as you do something about it. What's not okay is for you to stay in a job for one minute longer than absolutely necessary when you have fallen out of love with your fans. You owe yourself and the fans more than surface-level lip service. You owe them your total loyalty, enthusiasm, and good will.

In addition to being a superfan of your fans, you must also be a fan of the following:

1. **Your industry.** Are you a superfan of your industry? Do you believe that your product or service truly enriches the lives of your fans? Do you look forward to celebrating with peers in your industry and strive to promote the industry to others?

2. **Your company.** Are you a superfan of your company? Do you believe in the mission and purpose of the company you work for? Do you like the people you work with (on most days)? Do you believe that the products or services your company sells are best in class and worth investing in?

3. **Your profession.** Are you a superfan of sales as a profession? Can you honestly say that you love being a salesperson? Do you believe selling is a noble profession? Do you still get a thrill when your client signs a purchase agreement?

If any of these pieces are missing for you, then do something about it. Either learn how to fall in love again with your fans, industry, company, and/or your profession, or make a change.

REMEMBER YOUR WHY

Even the most ardent superfans have bad days. Just because you have a bad day here or there doesn't make you less of a superfan. It just makes you human. I know from personal experience that some days at work are better than others. I love my job. I can't believe that people actually pay me to talk and write books. It's a dream job. But when I'm sitting on the tarmac at midnight after a two-hour flight delay and I've been up since 5 a.m. that morning teaching a sales class all day—well, let's just say I'm not much of a superfan in that moment. What helps me, and what I hope will help you, is to remember your *why*.

We all have a *why*. Your *why* is the reason you work so hard. Your *why* motivates you to blow past your sales goals and win the company-wide sales contest. Your *why* helps you get up in the dark and leave work in the dark during cold winter months. Your *why* keeps your temper in check when fans are being unreasonable. Your *why* gets you through difficult conversations with your boss and your *why* rejoices when fans are truly satisfied.

You have a *why*. What is it? Maybe you have more than one. What's important is that on difficult or challenging days you tap into your why. Simply visualize it in your mind and take a deep breath. Focus on it for a moment and breathe. Close your eyes (as long as you aren't driving). Be still. Stop talking.

You and your *why* are a team. Together you can get through the most difficult of days, weeks, or seasons.

REMEMBER THEIR WHY

Guess what? Your fans have a *why*. Not only does tapping into your *why* help you manage difficult situations, it also helps you connect with your fans. When you can tap into your own *why*, it serves as a reminder that your fans have a *why*.

At the end of the day we all want the same things. We want a beautiful life. We want a life filled with meaningful relationships. We want health and happiness for our friends and loved ones. We want financial security. We want to explore new ideas and places. We want to learn and grow. We want to be happy and fulfilled.

How we express those things may be wildly different, but in the end, you have a *why*, and your fans have a *why*. Show your fans through your words and actions that you genuinely care about their *why* and you become the epitome of all that is FANtastic.

IN CONCLUSION

As you read through these ten important traits to becoming a FANtastic salesperson, what you will notice is the importance of understanding your fans and their place within the sales journey. Put yourself in their place and think about how you would want to be treated every step of the way. I've told you about numerous salespeople who have either lost my business or blown me away and made me a lifelong fan as a result of their approach to the art of selling. So when you plan your next call, presentation, or any engagement, think about how you would feel on the receiving end. Not only will you and your fans enjoy the interaction more, you will soon recognize yourself as that rock-star, top-producing, quota-busting salesperson you always knew you could be!

FORMULATE YOUR GAME PLAN

Five FANtastic Questions to Help You Become a Superfan

---

1. What is your *why*?

2. How do you show your fans that you care? List three of your superfan actions/behaviors.

3. Which one of the 10 undeniable traits resonated most with you? Which one resonated the least?

_____

_____

_____

_____

_____

_____

_____

_____

4. List three actions you want and need to take to become more FANtastic. What is your timeframe to achieve each action and who is going to support your efforts?

_____

_____

_____

_____

_____

_____

_____

_____

5. Regarding Question #4, what obstacles will you encounter and how do you plan to overcome those?

_____

_____

_____

_____

_____

_____

_____

_____

Quick View Summary of Game Plan Questions

TRAIT #1—RELEVANT

1. What does being relevant mean to you?
2. What is the first step you need to take to become more relevant to your buyers?
3. Think of an example of a relevant salesperson you've encountered recently. What did he/she say or do that made you feel like the conversation was relevant to you?
4. What is stopping you from becoming more relevant with your buyers?
5. What does a relevant conversation look like with your buyers and how do you know if you've achieved it?

TRAIT #2—INSIGHTFUL

1. What does being an insightful salesperson mean to you?

2. How do you normally communicate context? What does that sound like?

3. Which of the six categories of distinction—Price, Product, Process, People, Promotion and/or Purpose—apply to your product? Your company? To you personally?

4. Which of the context clues are you currently using (*So What, Why, Because*)? Which one(s) do you want to start using that you are not using now?

5. What does an insightful conversation look like with your buyers and how do you know if you've achieved it?

TRAIT #3—INQUISITIVE

1. What does being an inquisitive salesperson mean to you?

2. What is the difference between inquisitive and nosy? How do you strike a balance?

3. List one question you frequently are asked in each phase of the buying journey.

    Awareness—

    Consideration—

    Decision—

4. Approximately how many questions do you ask during a typical sales conversation? What steps do you need to take to ask more questions?

5. What is your favorite question that guarantees a response nearly every time you ask it? Share it with me at Meredith@ CreatingWOW.com.

TRAIT #4—ENGAGING

1. Think of an example of someone you find very engaging. It could be someone you know personally, or an athlete, celebrity, or political figure. What does that person say and/or do that you find so engaging?

2. How difficult is it for you to stay engaged and focused during conversations and meetings with your fans? Are you doing something else while the other person is talking?

3. What's stopping you from being fully present, engaged, and paying attention during sales conversations?

4. Imagine for a moment you are the client. What type of personalization would be meaningful to you?

5. If you were going to coach a salesperson on being engaging, what would your number one tip be?

TRAIT #5—AUTHENTIC

1. What is more of a challenge for you: 1) Letting people in to get to know the real you or 2) Maintaining professional boundaries to ensure an appropriate level of authenticity for the workplace?

2. Of the four trust breakers mentioned, which one do you struggle with the most? What is one action step you could take to improve that behavior?

3. In addition to the four trust breakers mentioned, what other trust breakers have you observed salespeople committing? What impact did that have on the relationship with their fans?

4. List three of your most trusted brands. What did they do or say to earn and keep your trust?

5. Imagine you found yourself in a situation similar to what I described at the very beginning of this chapter. What sales-related skills and experiences could you draw upon to de-escalate and resolve the situation?

TRAIT #6—NURTURING

1. Do you need to focus more on responding more quickly to leads, customizing your message to the fans, or adding more follow-up attempts to your process?

2. Do you have a CRM system? If yes, how do you really feel about it? Can you consider the possibility it could be a Cash Recovery Machine for you if used properly or fully? What is one action step that needs to happen for you to be able to use it more fully?

3. If you answered no to Question #2, what is one action step you need to take to implement a CRM system, either for yourself personally or for your company?

4. What is your current follow-up process? How many times do you typically continue to follow up after an initial conversation? Is that current process working for you? What is your current follow-up response rate?

5. What communication channel do you prefer? How rigid or how flexible are you in regard to using other channels? Is there a channel you need to learn more about or become more familiar with so you can use it when needed?

TRAIT #7—SOCIABLE

1. What social media channels are your fans using? How did you come to those conclusions?

2. Are you consistently posting on social media? What percentage of your posts are sales versus non-sales messages?

3. What is your favorite type of content on social media? What do you gravitate toward? How could you include that type of content for your business?

4. What does "the art of the shout-out" mean to you? How could you use that on social media to build relationships with your fans?

5. Tweet me a shout-out @MeredithCSP with the #FANtasticSelling hashtag and I will tweet right back at you!

TRAIT #8—EFFICIENT

1. What percentage of your day is spent on sales activities (lead nurturing, prospecting, networking) versus non-sales activities (administrative tasks, meetings, and emails)?

2. What is one action you could take today to spend more time on sales activities (without neglecting your other work)? When will you take that action?

3. On a scale from 1 to 5 (5 being a technology Jedi Master and 1 being a caveman trying to learn how to start a fire with flint), how comfortable are you with technology, your CRM, your smartphone, and apps?

4. If you scored a 1 to 3 on Question #3, what is one action you need to take to become a solid 4 or 5 on the technology comfort and usage rating scale? When will you take that action?

5. Send me an email at meredith@creatingwow.com with your favorite app and why. I would love to hear from you what apps make a difference in your professional or personal life.

TRAIT #9—PREPARED

1. Make a list of three skills, attitudes, or behaviors that you need to learn more about.
2. What is one action you could take to learn more about the three items you listed in Question #1?
3. Determine your PDB, Personal Development Budget, number. What is that number based on? How will you ensure that money is available to you throughout the year and doesn't get spent elsewhere?
4. Are you a member of your local industry association? If not, research local associations and select one to join. Join in the next 30 days. If yes, what is the next educational event you could attend? Schedule that event on your calendar and get registered for it. No excuses!
5. Send me an email at meredith@creatingwow.com with your favorite podcast or TED talk. I would love to hear what you listen to and watch to stay motivated.

TRAIT #10—SUPERFAN

1. What is your *why*?
2. How do you show your fans that you care? List three of your superfan actions/behaviors.
3. Which one of the 10 undeniable traits resonated most with you? Which one resonated the least?

4. List three actions you want and need to take to become more FANtastic. What is your timeframe to achieve each action and who is going to support your efforts?

5. Regarding Question #4, what obstacles will you encounter and how do you plan to overcome those?

Have Meredith Speak at Your Next Event

LOOKING FOR A PROFESSIONAL SPEAKER to WOW your audience? Meredith Oliver is the answer!

Inspirational, fun, and relevant, Meredith Oliver is a sales and marketing keynote speaker, author, and strategist who works with businesses wanting to capitalize on the Fan Factor. Meredith isn't just another self-proclaimed sales and marketing keynote speaker; she has fifteen years of experience creating and delivering effective digital marketing campaigns that lead to more sales. She is the founder and president of Meredith Communications, a digital marketing agency located in Raleigh, North Carolina. Meredith Communications specializes in website development, search engine optimization, and social media marketing.

Meredith has spoken to audiences ranging in size from 10 to 2,000 at prominent industry events, such as the International

Builders Show and the Annual Conference of the National Automobile Dealers Association. She holds the prestigious designation of Certified Speaking Professional®, the highest credential conferred by the National Speakers Association.

Book Meredith for your next event and treat your audience to a dynamic, fun, powerhouse program packed with practical information. Here's what audience members and event planners have to say about Meredith's appearances.

"What might be one of her most engaging qualities as a speaker is her ability to connect with the audience in a real and personal way."
SmartMeetings Magazine, December 2015

"Your presentation was fabulous! I have had so many compliments from my members and participants about the presentation; so much so, that everyone wants a repeat performance. So, look forward to coming back to Kansas City. We want you back!"
Dawn Allen, Director of Education, Kansas City Home Builders Association

"Thank you Meredith! You definitely hit a home run with my client."
Angela Cox-Weston, Midwest Speakers Bureau

"I have seen and frequently hired just about every sales/marketing trainer/speaker in the business, and after seeing your presentation tonight, I would say you are among the very best."
Gib Dickey, Publisher Atlanta Communities Magazine

Connect with Meredith

MeredithCommunications.com
Meredith Speaks.com
Twitter: @MeredithCSP
Instagram: @MeredithsShoes22
Facebook.com/MeredithCommunications
LinkedIn.com/in/MeredithOliver
YouTube.com/MeredithOliverTV

Endnotes

1   Baron, Eric. "Selling is a Team Sport: Turn Your Whole Organization into a Living, Breathing, Selling Machine." 2000. http://amzn.to/2gRw8a3.

2   Morrison, Kimberlee. "81% of Shoppers Conduct Online Research Before Buying." *AdWeek*. 28 November 2014. http://bit.ly/2geLcgB.

3   Sullivan, Laurie. "70% of Consumers Use Three Channels or More To Research A Purchase." *Mediapost*. 27 October 2015. http://bit.ly/2fxjay3.

4   Manoukian, Julia. "The Rise of the Modern Salesperson [Infographic]." *SalesForLife*. 19 October 2016. http://bit.ly/2fHi2D8.

5   Guglielmi, Valeria. "3 Marketing Lessons from the 'Share a Coke' Campaign." *MayeCreate Design*. 7 May. http://bit.ly/1LoT8Yb.

6   McQuilken, Toni. "'Share a Coke' Campaign Grows Sales For The First Time in 10 Years, WSJ reports." *AdWeek*. 26 September 2014. http://bit.ly/2gBDde7.

7   Tarver, Eric. "What Makes the 'Share a Coke' Campaign So Successful?" *Investopedia*. 7 October 2015. http://bit.ly/2fHo7PQ.

8   Oliver, Meredith. "FANtastic Marketing: Leverage Your Fan Factor, Build a Blockbuster Brand, Score New Customers, and

Wipe Out the Competition." 2016.
https://www.amazon.com/dp/B01LY1X0IJ.

9   Solomon, Micah. "2016 Is The Year Of The Millennial Customer: Is Your Customer Experience Ready?" *Forbes.com*. 14 November 2105. http://bit.ly/2g12HhE.

10 Bialik, Carl. "Starbucks Stays Mum on Drink Math." *Wall Street Journal Blog*. 2 April 2008. http://on.wsj.com/1EYTGww.

11 Smith, Aaron. "U.S. Smartphone Use in 2015." *PewResearch Center*. 1 April 2015. http://pewrsr.ch/19JDwMd.

12 "Dove Campaign for Real Beauty." *Wikipedia*. 29 November 2016. http://bit.ly/2aeb7hX.

13 Morales, Stephanie. "Reader's Digest Announces 2016's Trusted Brands." *Trusted Media Brands*. 20 September 2016. http://bit.ly/2g114R1.

14 London, Stacy. "The Truth About Style." 2013. http://amzn.to/2gRuPYF.

15 Williams, Margery. "The Velveteen Rabbit." 1958. http://amzn.to/2gs489k.

16 Offenberger, Brian. "20 Crucial Sales Stats Every Salesperson Should Know." *SDM Magazine*. 2 December 2015. http://bit.ly/2fMbAOi.

17 Rosauer, Kelsey. "7 Surprising Sales Statistics & What To Do About Them." *Agency Bloc*. 23 June 2106. http://bit.ly/2e4erjc.

18 "Shocking Sales Statistics As It Relates To Follow Up." *FollowUpSuccess.com*. 21 February 2011. http://bit.ly/1niou2n.

19 Atwood, Jake. "20 Shocking Sales Stats: Knowing Them Will Change How You Sell." *Slideshare.com*. 10 September 2103. http://bit.ly/1f9Ve9u.

20 Atwood, Jake. "20 Shocking Sales Stats: Knowing Them Will Change How You Sell." *Slideshare.com*. 10 September 2103. http://bit.ly/1f9Ve9u.

21   Ward, Chris. "Customer Service Departments Leave 50% of Online Queries Unanswered." *MyCustomer.com*. 5 March 2015. http://bit.ly/2fMavWJ.

22   Krogue, Ken. "Why Companies Waste 71% of Internet Leads." *Forbes.com*. 12 July 2012. http://bit.ly/2fM7Mws.

23   "The Lead Response Management Study." *LeadResponseManagement. org*. 29 November 2016. http://bit.ly/1o8Azrm.

24   Oldrody, James. "The Short Life of Online Sales Leads." *Harvard Business Review*. March 2011. http://bit.ly/1vNDmeV.

25   Atwood, Jake. "20 Shocking Sales Stats: Knowing Them Will Change How You Sell." *Slideshare.com*. 10 September 2103. http://bit.ly/1f9Ve9u.

26   "Shocking Sales Statistics As It Relates To Follow Up." *FollowUpSuccess.com*. 21 February 2011. http://bit.ly/1niou2n.

27   Greenwood, Shannon. Perrin, Andrew. Duggan, Maeve. "Social Media Update 2016." PewResearch Center. 11 November 2016. http://pewrsr.ch/2fIeTTY.

28   Byers Settle, Hillary. "The Key to Social Selling is Social, Not Selling." Convince & Convert. http://bit.ly/1H6MAGt.

29   "Rich Real Estate Agent, Poor Real Estate Agent." *Active Rain*. 9 November 2011. http://bit.ly/2fMmIL1.

30   "Rich Real Estate Agent, Poor Real Estate Agent." *Active Rain*. 9 November 2011. http://bit.ly/2fMmIL1.

31   "State of Sales in 2016." *LinkedIn Sales Solutions*. 29 November 2016. http://bit.ly/28PsCtD.

32   Horrigan, John. "Lifelong Learning & Technology." *PewResearch Center*. 22 March 2016. http://pewrsr.ch/21FgYAE

33   Tracy, Brian. "Discover The Importance of Lifelong Learning." Brian Tracy International. http://bit.ly/1iTsSah.

Made in the USA
Middletown, DE
06 May 2017